Conversations at the Well

Conversations at the Well

Emerging Religious Life in the 21st-Century Global World:
Collaboration, Networking, and Intercultural Living

Jung Eun Sophia Park, SNJM
WITH Tere Maya, CCVI

FOREWORD BY
Pat Farrell, OSF

WIPF & STOCK · Eugene, Oregon

CONVERSATIONS AT THE WELL
Emerging Religious Life in the 21st-Century Global World: Collaboration, Networking, and Intercultural Living

Wipf & Stock
An Imprint of Wipf and Stock Publishers
199 W. 8th Ave., Suite 3
Eugene, OR 97401

www.wipfandstock.com

PAPERBACK ISBN: 978-1-5326-4977-6
HARDCOVER ISBN: 978-1-5326-4978-3
EBOOK ISBN: 978-1-5326-4979-0

Manufactured in the U.S.A.   08/19/19

Contents

Foreword

PAT FARRELL, OSF

I resonate deeply with what is written in these pages. Having lived many years of my life in international missions, I know the transformative potential, the risk, and the vulnerability of liminal space, hybrid identity, and marginality. It is a great gift. I know the challenge of finding a home in the in-between places and I cherish the gift of hospitality. I recognize my own life in the words of the authors: "When we consider liminal space, embracing the other means encountering our own deep darkness, shedding our own ideas and assumptions, and letting the other guide us." That rings so true!

The authors carry interculturality in the very fabric of their beings. From that graced perspective they speak boldly of the future of religious life. Their writing combines scholarship and theory with reflection on lived experience and is born of dialogue that reflects encounter, diversity, and collaboration.

I appreciate their respectful inclusivity amid ideological tensions dotting the current landscape of US religious life. Additionally, the historical perspective offered here is not iconoclastic. Reflecting on the last century of apostolic religious life with its repeated attempts to domesticate an essentially prophetic lifestyle, the authors point to liberating impulses throughout. It segues into their innovative look at the future of religious life.

The question of that future is nothing new. This book, nonetheless, addresses the issue with freshness and hope. Rather than focusing on diminishment, however real, it directs our attention to the transformation already budding, quietly, in the experience of newer members of religious congregations. Those women are already living into a newness largely unarticulated, mostly still invisible, impossible to capture with language from the past. Theirs is the task of creating space and language for that newness, of noticing where and when it erupts, of moving towards it together through encounter and dialogue. Truly, this is a moment of grace.

The emergent future comes subtly and unobtrusively. When the old falls away the new simply shows itself, a somewhat startling recognition. In some ways it is like coming home to what has been there all along. The difference is our ability to see it when we are no longer blinded by the familiar. The authors refer to a "very gradual clearing . . ."

What, then, is new? The context, certainly. The world of new members to religious life is one of globalization, neoliberal capitalism, and multicultural societies. There is growing diversity among them in age, culture, language, and race. They come with skills for connection and communication common to those born into an electronic age.

Encounter as a way of engaging the ever-changing reality of the present would seem a natural, spontaneous response for them. To a degree, I believe it is. We see surfacing in the recent cohort of religious life with our lives a great deal of collaboration, networking, creativity, mutuality, equality, high mobility, flexibility, ease with uncertainty, a contemplative spirit, and a leaning toward horizontal and networked leadership. Therein lies a glimpse of how the future might be unfolding. However, such a way forward does not happen without conscious choice. Even as they experience greater diversity, multiculturalism, and hybrid identities, newer members must decide the degree to which they will embrace the liminality in which they are immersed. All of us are ultimately faced with that challenge.

One of the significant contributions of this book is its structure of storytelling, weaving a lovely scriptural thread with the image of the women at the well. Through that story it articulates the value of standing on the margins, creating a culture of encounter, and elaborating a new narrative of religious life from there. "People of liminality can only hold power if they gain voices to articulate their position." This book is one such voice. It begins to articulate a position and invites the empowerment of further expression.

Whatever new expression we give to it, religious life will always be a way of living into the inner freedom of the Gospel. It will always be a following of Jesus the Christ. It will continue to call us to risk taking and vulnerable love, discernment and deep listening, contemplation and conversion. Yet changing circumstances call us to give new expression to what is of the essence. This historical moment of massive displacement of peoples and the global crisis of millions of immigrants and refugees calls religious life to speak a new word with our lives. "The religious can bring 'otherness' in our church and communities out of invisibility and into conversation." We can deepen the capacity to live our mission interculturally and to grow in being a vocation for justice in a global world. We can break open new dimensions of intercultural living for a world desperately in need of it. What you are about to read inspires that journey.

Acknowledgements

This book is all about friendship, which has buoyed my spiritual journey of women religious in the US. I acknowledge that this book on the emerging religious life in the twenty-first century in the global world lies on the spirit of networking, collaboration, and mutual transformation. With this spirit, I hope anyone would join in these conversations at the well, which represents a space of dialogue by sharing in reflections and conversations, and the conversations would be continued and bear fruits. Also, this book is interdisciplinary, in which diverse discourses from cultural studies, postcolonial theory, psychological theory, as well as the field of management sociology are appropriated. In so doing, this book extends our theological scope and affirms that our discourse exists concretely within the world.

One of the main conversation partners for this book was Sr. Tere Maya, CCVI, who brought a variety of references from Latin America, including Mexico and Argentina. Her engagement and dialogues with various religious communities and theologians from Latin America, which was shared with me, gave a vivid sense of liberation and lived reality of the global South. Tere was born in Mexico and educated in the United States. Her constant border crossings between the United States and Mexico were sealed when her religious institutes were reconfigured from the separate US and Latin-American units into a single level of governance. She has focused on bridging the different cultures of her congregation and inviting institutes around the world to embrace their interculturality as a moment of grace. In 2016 she was elected to the LCWR (Leadership Conference of Women Religious) presidency. Her background is in history and education, but her leadership roles have given her great passion for religious life and encouraged her to challenge leaders of religious institutes to work intentionally for the future of a life form with much to offer our world and society. My conversations with her brought me, who is trained as theologian in the US, a more balanced view of religious life in the twenty-first century. From the beginning of the project to the completion, Teresa has been a great part of this book project as a dialogue partner.

The other conversation partner that I cherish is Sr. Mary Pat LeRoy, SNJM, who has served her community as a leader, critical thinker, and wisdom figure. She gave me always very broad reading lists with great challenge and encouragement. One day, Sr. Mary Pat told me that she would die in the desert serving the old generation, like perhaps Miriam, Moses, and Aaron, while I would go to the promised land. I pondered over and over again what she said, and I confess her deep wisdom helped me to cross over a boundary and to explore the theme of religious life in the twenty-first century in a sense of freedom.

The last, but not the least dialogue partner is Sr. Julia Prinz, VDMF, a German-American sister. We met as doctoral students in Christian Spirituality at Graduate Theological Union and discussed the vision of religious life in a global perspective. Her contemplative-active vision has inspired me always.

For this book project, I deeply appreciate many sisters and friends who live in US and in other countries in the globe such as Vietnam, China, Korea, Bolivia, Peru, Malaysia, and Lesotho. Finally, I thank my Holy Names University students, who were willingly engaged in conversations and dialogues with me about emerging religious life.

Finally, I appreciate Eunice Park and Nancy Hunt, who read my manuscript carefully and corrected errors as well as suggesting better ways of articulation.

I do not know what is the future of the religious life, yet I know there is a religious vocation called by God on the mission. It is clear that women religious are grounded on and led by the legacy of the Jesus movement as the subject of interpretation which is open to the future. As long as we continue to dialogue with others, we will find always new and alternative lifestyles, claiming gospel values. By relinking the people on the globe, we will walk into the future in the spirit of freedom and comfort in the journey of religious life.

Introduction

Wake up the world!
Be the witness of a different way of acting, of living
It is possible to live differently in this world . . .
It is this witness I expect from you!

—"Rejoice!: A Letter to Consecrated Men and Women"
by Pope Francis

Desire itself is movement
Not in itself desirable;
Love is itself unmoving,
Only the cause and end of movement,

. . .

Quick now, here, now, always
Ridiculous that waste sad time
Stretching before and after.

—"Burnt Norton" by T. S. Elliot

C onversations about religious life in the United States invariably end with the question, *What is the future of religious life?"* This question holds everything, from the profound uncertainty that this form of life is disappearing to a resilient conviction that transformation is necessary. The numbers game that has been prevalent in assessing the American church implies a sense of failure because of the narrative of diminishment that has cast a shadow over religious institutions for the last several decades. Questions about the future are further compounded by the ideological tension that has polarized our church and even this conversation. The decrease in actual numbers has been used to justify the judgment of communities that embraced the renewal of the Vatican Council with singular zeal and to praise the communities that chose a more traditional path into the future. How useful has this narrative been in explaining the subtle transformation that has taken place? How can this narrative explain that women religious are called to their charisms and mission? While questions about the future focus almost exclusively on the faithful task of completion, a subtle and quiet transformation has been taking place in religious congregations across the United States.

Women religious often have conversations about what diversity means and how it can transform religious life in ways we cannot even imagine. We might navigate the transition of many institutions and the faithful passing of the large cohorts of sisters from the Great Generation, who have left active ministry as they enter their eighties. There is indeed a crisis of the religious life that we have become accustomed to, and significant numbers of sisters running Catholic schools and hospitals or a significant presence in direct service with the poor becomes a sight out of the past.

In grace, nevertheless, communities face their aging and declining numbers with courage and faithfulness. Many will continue to move into the completion of their mission and will consider other options for canonical governance because they lack members who can serve in leadership roles. They will appoint canonical superiors from other institutions, who are called commissaries.[1] Even in this dismal reality, a new wave of collaboration and a deeper understanding of transformation in the faith are already breathing a new way of religious life among us.

At this juncture, we must raise the question of whether women religious—particularly apostolic women religious—have a future in the United States. We recognize that the past exists as a virtual reality yet occupies the heart of the present; we note the future exists only as a vision that emerges from critical and mystical contemplation. Thus, the question is directly related to the vision of our mission in the world today. The rapid transformation of our

1. Resource Center for Religious Institutes, "Q and A," 4–6.

institution and the move into completion and smaller numbers have created a space for new conversations.

We know that we must address our legacy in terms of ministries and institutions, but at the same time we are aware that the future will require a fresh new outlook on mission and presence. How do we notice what is already happening among us? How do we appreciate what is coming to life in the midst of grief and loss?

People who are nostalgic about the "good old days" wonder where the sisters have gone (and hopefully miss them). The perennial debate over the visibility of women religious offers comfort for those who long for habits and the rows of sisters filling into large convents in secluded locations. These kinds of visuals are part of an old narrative that often polarizes conversations. Mass media, Hollywood, and even Catholic pundits often return to the imagery of "nuns in habits." Often this image of the habit is understood as the essential identity of women religious.[2] However, we cannot afford to spend more time on a debate about externals when we are called to notice what is emerging, to bless the next generation, and to trust with faith that all our lives have not been in vain. We have been called into God's love, and God will not judge us by the clothes we wear but rather by the love we bear. The identity of women religious cannot rest solely on their clothes. Whether in a habit, uniform, simple clothes, or professional clothes—we are all one in our heart for our mission.

The emerging new understanding and identity of religious life lies on our storytelling, and women religious—both in and out of the habit—need to share our lived stories of faithfulness. We need to share the heart of our lives from different perspectives in which we have been living out the revolutionary vision of the Second Vatican Council.

When we stop to take stock of the fantastic stories that have woven together the current religious life and seek to explore the meaning that brought all of us—from every corner of the theological divide—and share our more profound stories of communion and transformation in God, we will notice the quiet, gentle

2. Park, "Religious Life in the U.S.," 47–53.

transformation that God has initiated among us. Perhaps when we have had our debates and clashes over different ideas, when we have left nostalgia behind, wiping away tears of grief and fear of loss, then we might notice the fresh breath of God gently breaking the dawn and lifting the fog.

Then we will remain free to embrace what is coming and to ask the required question of every generation, "*Who is next?*" Moreover, if we are hopeful enough and willing to let go of the boundaries that, we believe, would keep safely the religious life, we will notice, celebrate, and welcome the women who are being called to our charisms. There is a generation on the horizon that would continue this legacy in a new way. They will be small in number, but they are the ones who will enter into a new challenging reality. They are daughters of their time, having been born into the realities of globalization and neoliberal capitalism amid multicultural societies. Their religious vowed life, community, and mission need to be situated and understood in this context.

This book is an exploration and reflection of the life of women religious that is emerging in the United States in the context of a global world. Several studies have demonstrated its growing challenges along with the greater diversity in the professional fields that women religious serve and the increasing numbers of international sisters serving in the United States.[3] We are also being called to live into greater interculturality, something we have diligently tried to learn.[4] As well-known missionary scholar Anthony Gittins suggests, "The future of religious life will depend on our capacity to live mission interculturally."[5] The perspectives and experiences of the international and intercultural religious who are serving in the United States will contribute to the future of religious life. Also, there will be an increasing need to articulate the core values of religious life in the twenty-first century, located in the midst of a

---

3. Johnson et al., *New Generations of Catholic Sisters*, 256.

4. Catholic Theological Union and Religious Formation Conference offered workshops, emphasizing the cultural diversity in religious life.

5. See Gittins, *Living Mission Interculturally.*

global world, which focus on the mission of living out a passion and compassion for the world.[6]

What is emerging is still tentative and far from clarity, yet women religious know that there is no such reality without dialogue and conversation. We have ample lived experiences already unfolding in the religious life that have not yet burgeoned into discourse. Often I am fascinated by the fact that many aspects of religious life are not fully articulated as well as by the realization that existing narratives do not echo the lived experiences of the *newly unfolding* religious life.

These new emerging narratives are about a new reality of religious life in the United States—one that is much more diverse in terms of age, culture, language, and race, and more vigorous in the context of collaboration, networking, and creativity. I often run into this reality sometimes while offering workshops for the Giving Voice Sisters' national gathering or the Religious Formation Conference programs, and other times while hearing about the international sisters in the newly created ALHMA (Asociación de Hermanas Latinas Misioneras en America) or the FSVN (Foundation for Sisters from Vietnam). These increased interests, concerns, and conversations about multiculturality in religious life have been our experience, reflection, and discernment.

Further, I am encouraged by the effect the 2016 presentation by Dr. Shannen Dee Williams at the LCWR assembly created.[7] This growing awareness of racism in our institutions was further kindled by the fiftieth celebration of the National Black Sisters Conference in New Orleans in July 2018. After such a long journey, our religious institutions are addressing the racism within us with a level of honesty and realism that gives us hope.

The book *In Our Own Words: Sharing the Voices of Younger Women Religious*, which offers reflections of religious life in the United States, has opened up spaces for conversation around our growing diversity. The Global Sisters Report, a project of the

---

6. I recognize the efforts of theologians, sociologists, and historians in this regard.

7. Araujo-Hawkins, "Reckoning," para. 4.

National Catholic Reporter launched in 2016, has inspired me, as it pays attention to the voices of young sisters from around the globe. In addition, global networking such as the Women Wisdom and Action program, run by Julia Prinz, VDF, for eight years (2011–2019), which focused on American women religious theologians' collaborations with sisters who are doing theology in Asia, also shed light on this emerging paradigm for religious life.

Beyond the United States, I find women religious speaking of the need for greater collaboration in every area of ministry. At a gathering in Bangkok, Thailand, fifty women religious from the US and various countries of Asia talked about religious life and the vocation for justice in the global world. UISG (International Union Superiors General) has quickly become a great supporter of these conversations. I find women religious around the globe committed to collaboration, which was not common in earlier years. This passion demonstrates the genuine need for today's mission as well as for a spirit of mutuality and equality in the conversation; it is no longer just a "north to south" conversation with a domineering West.

Conversations have evolved over the last few years as I personally struggled in understanding the meaning of religious life in the United States. In exchanging ideas, hopes, and concerns with other sisters, I have experienced the transformation of the conversations that initially brought people together and connect one another deeply and strongly.

We women religious are supposed to gather at the well, a space for conversation, because we find "*living water*" and a hope for a future of the religious life we have embraced and loved. At the well, each conversation partner brings her own life story and perspective, including joy, sorrow, and hope. Over the years, the friendships and conversations have been the fundamental principles behind this book project.

As a Korean immigrant whose passion and ministry is teaching religious studies with an emphasis on interfaith and interspirituality, I have engaged with young people from various cultures and ethnicities. My own journey in religious life began when I joined a Korean congregation in 1990. Through the formation and ministry, I experienced a semi-cloistered monastic apostolic religious life. Eventually, the study of theology in the US transformed my passion for religious life, and since then my spiritual inquiry has been the true identity and lifestyle of women religious. In other words, my question has been, "*What is the essence of apostolic religious life?*"

It was a necessary and essential process for me to sit with sisters and friends to converse about who we are and where we are going. It is the very narrative of the Samaritan woman who had a bold dialogue with a stranger (John 4). The well is a symbol of encounter, newness, fertility, and the mission of religious life. In the biblical tradition, the well signifies the event of encountering the significant other as a stranger. In Genesis, Rebecca meets a stranger who will guide her to her husband. Rachel meets Jacob, who comes to love her more than anyone else.

The well is a space to fundamentally open up to everyone, to experience transformation through encounter, and to regain vitality through water. This book is the fruit of two and half years' worth of conversations over dinner tables in convent guest houses as meditations and reflections at the well, where all elements of religious life are shared and prayed over. It is true that "in the beginning was religious life" as a lived experience, and I chewed, digested, and understood what it meant to be us, *now and here* with my friends and sisters.

The approach of this book, thus, is fundamentally dialogical. Since the Second Vatican Council, women religious have been the ardent and faithful constituency of the church as the people of God, who have embodied the spirit in every aspect of life. As Margaret Brennan, IHM, indicated, women religious in the United States as early as the 1970s proclaimed their desire to stand against the dominant culture of consumerism and its power to alienate and to destroy humanity. Women religious in the US have been recognized as a collaborative group that has pursued alternative ways to reflect on society's prevailing mores.[8] As women religious

8. LCWR, "History," para. 1.

have been evolving in this direction, this book considers how alternative ways of collaboration could happen. A new way is already among those of us who are talking together, and the way requires that we encourage one another to "perceive it." Look, the new shoot of the trunk . . . (Isaiah 43).

Religious life, as it exists in its current reality, is located in liminal space. Nancy Schreck, OSF, addressed the LCWR assembly in 2014, calling leaders to recognize that we were in the "middle space."[9] While it may seem like we have been here for a long time, we are actually moving close to dawn. However, we must first understand liminal space in order to indicate the "in-between space," with an emphasis neither on *this* (naming the past or old model of religious life) nor *that* (naming the future of religious life), yet with a great possibility for transformation and production.

Anthropologist Victor Turner explains liminal space in his study of ritual as that which negates the current structure and seeks an alternative way to liberate and transform the current situation. Furthermore, Catherine Bell, a scholar of ritual studies, elaborates on liminal space, characterizing it as the function of an anti-narrative to subvert social order. Often language functions to cooperate with the social order, which complies with the institution, the nation, and the church. Thus, liminal space (or the narrative of the liminal space) creates an anti-narrative and, in so doing, either negates the main oppressive narrative of the given society or creates a new narrative to provide a new perspective.[10] As an example, in South East Asia, one should not step on the threshold of a dwelling because the threshold signifies the in-between space—already started but not yet come—which is where the divine dwells. When religious women seek understanding and clear vision on the ground of the liminal space, we stand on holy ground, where the Spirit can guide us.

When I say religious women live and serve in liminal space, I am not referring only to historical transitions. Instead, I mean that we live in the reality of a multicultural and interreligious world,

9. Schreck, "However Long the Night," para. 5–6.
10. See Bell, *Ritual Theory; Theory Ritual.*

engaging with others and residing on the margin spiritually and socially, often even physically. Also, I assume that apostolic women religious in the United States are all participants in the Jesus movement, for the kingdom of God, wherein everyone journeys as a disciple of Jesus, who resides among the people and dreams of an alternative world of friendship and mutual empowerment.

Finally, apostolic religious life has changed according to the times and needs of the world. In this way, I dream of marching into a life-giving future, creating an alternative view set against the current crises of global capitalism, ecological destruction, poverty, and massive numbers of refugees.[11]

My primary dialogue partner, Sr. Tere Maya, who has much understanding of religious life in the US as the president of LCWR as well as the leader of her religious community, CCVI, has provided me with great insights and ample knowledge. Her vision for the intercultural future and deep theological sources from Latin America extended my vision.

This book is composed of seven chapters:

Chapter 1, "Apostolic Religious Life as a Liminal Space in the Global World," elaborates on the concept of liminal space, where uncertainty and mingling function as sources of transformation and life. Here the feeling of fear through encountering the other and the possibility of hybrid identity will be acknowledged, and creativity and openness will be appreciated. Also, it sketches the unique pathway of US religious women as residents of liminal space as a way to project our future.

In chapter 2, "Remapping the World," I attempt to remap the cultural landscape amid our emerging reality. Understanding the United States as a crossroads of diversity can help us frame the conversation about what is emerging in twenty-first-century religious life. This new map analyzes the global world, paying attention to people's experience of dislocation and various alternative views on the world. The suggested intercultural living is not just an idea, but a vivid reality that needs to be explored more.

---

11. Harmer, *Religious Life in the 21ˢᵗ Century*, 21.

In chapter 3, I examine "The Jesus Movement," which originated with Jesus of Galilee and was developed by the disciples who returned to Galilee in the light of resurrection. The earthly Jesus lived in first-century Palestine, at the crossroads of the Roman Empire, which required a liminal way of living.[12] Religious life today invites us to revisit the Jesus movement through the lens of engagement with others, focusing on the human experience in the global world in order to understand how apostolic religious life can relate to the world.

In chapter 4, I explore "Vows: Living in Liminal Space," which demands an inner freedom to take risks for Gospel values, as participants in the Jesus movement. Revisiting the three vows, I focus on the multicultural and cross-cultural lives we now face. Each one of the vows has the possibility of breaking open a new dimension of intercultural living, to offer a prophetic stance that is desperately needed in the world today.

Chapter 5, "Spirituality of the Liminal Community," focuses on a renewed spirituality, requiring various boundary crossings. Here, I explore how the meaning of community can be extended by examining possible spirituality in community as a liminal space, which is fundamentally required to combine various elements. An emerging spirituality of community is introduced through the close reading of the New Testament. In Luke's Gospel 1:26–36 the meaning of "behold" and the literary structure of Acts are used respectively as an element of the liminal space and as a model of border crossing or intercultural community. Also, this chapter concludes with the spirituality of the liminal communities that can be summarized as the kenosis and the freedom of letting go and letting come.

Chapter 6, "Border-Crossing Leadership," is a search for a new style of leadership that does not operate as gatekeeper but rather leads members into the margins where mission flourishes. In this new way of leadership, openness to the other, as well as a spirituality marked by discernment and deep listening, will be required. As a small community, the leadership will be the shared leadership or

12. Elizondo, *Galilean Journey*, 57.

the shared governance in which each member takes a leadership role. An undeniable diversity will challenge our understanding of leadership and construct a horizontal and networked leadership that is able to multiply resources.

Sr. Tere Maya, in chapter 7, "Encounters in Today's Reality: The Art of Bridge Building and Bridge Crossing," uses beautiful poems about bridges, explaining how engagement with others enriches the ministry and the life of human beings as well as society. She employs the word *encuentro* as the central theme. In this chapter, Sr. Tere brings the notion of bridge crossing, citing the theology of *mestizaje* and the Aparecida document, which draws from the Fifth General Conference of the Bishops of Latin America and the Caribbean in 2007 as well as from Pope Francis's teachings on encounter for a vision of religious life.

In conclusion, I address a strong hope for the future of religious life, rooted in our charism and calling from Jesus. Throughout the conversations at the well, I have kindled our hope of living into the diversity emerging in religious life, as well as crossing borders in every possible way. In so doing, I feel a vibrant future for religious life is emerging. Diversity can reenergize charisms among us. Like organic living systems, religious life is nourished and sustained by diversity. This new way requires skills in connection and communication that new generations will surely bring, and this web of connectivity and energy will positively influence our religious life. In this book, I used the NRSV for biblical passages. When I use different version, I indicated it in the citation.

I sincerely hope that our mission will go forward into the global world of the twenty-first century. In the spirit of global sisterhood, we will continue the march of the Jesus movement with a deep desire for freedom, and all the sisters around the world can be in dialogue, learning together, to heed the call of the times.

_____

Chapter 2

Remapping the World

> Once
> by mistake
> she tore a map
> in hail.
> . . .
> There were mountains
> Righter next to her hometown.
> Wouldn't is that be nice
> If it were true?
> I'd tear a map
> And be right next
> to you.
>
> —"Torn Map" by Naomi Shihab Nye

> You live in a village where the other Koreans live.
> Same as you.
> Refugees. Immigrants. Exiles.
> Farther away from the land that is not your own.
> Not your own any longer.
>
> —"Dictée" by Theresa Hak Hyung Cha

There are many ways to draw a map. How then can we map the US in the global era? Understanding the United States as a crossroads where diverse people gather and live together would inspire us to frame an alternative religious life which is emerging in the twenty-first century. This new map would suggest intercultural living as an alternative way for the global world, which often enforces the same way of Western or American culture on other people. This intercultural life is not just an idea but rather a vivid reality that needs to be unpacked.

As the first step to draw the map of the US, I will describe a few elements that can characterize the word *globalization,* which is so pervasive that we seem to have various interpretations. However, it is clear we are all influenced by it. Thanks to advanced technology and the Internet, all information is shared by people who have access instantaneously. However, we fully are aware that not all enjoy the benefit of access; many people are left out of this loop and they experience much alienation and isolation as well as financial disadvantages.

Of importance in this dynamic is free-market capitalism, which goes along with globalization, and this reality creates global capitalism. Capital freely flows toward the direction in which the owners of the capital can maximize their benefit, and in this system people and resources are exploited. As a consequence, the level of damage to the ecological system is alarming, and we experience extreme weather and often natural disasters such as tsunamis and earthquakes, which challenge our consumer-centered lifestyle.

Also, while the few enjoy material wealth, most people live in poverty. In the system of neoliberalism, which is the system of financialized global capitalism, a human being is considered as a commodity or simple a piece of the labor force; very often human dignity is overlooked. It results in human rights problems on the global level, such as dislocation of refugees, immigration, and human trafficking. As a way of examining the global world, I will focus on the problem of human dislocation and on an alternative way of living, including the resistance movement, and will suggest a transformative way of intercultural living.

Dislocation

As revealed by the philosopher Martin Heidegger's term *unheimlich* or *unheimlichkeit,* dislocation literally designates "un-housed-ness" or "not-at-home-ness," a state that can be translated as "uncanny" or "uncanniness,"[1] connoting a situation of being outside of the "real" and "normal" experience. Dislocation does not mean merely homelessness but rather a lack of a space where a person can feel rooted and safe. Moreover, dislocation often implies a status of being on the edge or in liminal space, not only as a physical territory but also as an emotional and social territory. Often this space requires or produces a crossing of a person's own cultural or national boundary. In today's global world, the scale of dislocation is much more dramatic and violent. Let me explain three aspects of dislocation: exile, human trafficking, and immigration.

Exile

We remember the pictures of those who lost their land and homes from the wars in the Middle East, those waiting at the border for permission to cross as a way to go to Europe. In the summer of 2018, I conducted research on refugees from Yemen on Jeju island in South Korea. Young men from Yemen walking on the streets of the island provoked lots of discomfort among Jeju islanders because no one anticipated encountering refugees from the Arab continent.

Korea had accepted refugees from Vietnam after the Vietnam War, but the refugee camp in Busan was closed in 1995. Despite this experience, accepting Yemenese was more challenging because of Islamophobia, especially for very conservative Korean Christians, who were opposed to accepting them without full understanding. They feared that the influence of the refugees' religion would destroy their faith or that some of them might be ISIS member or terrorists. However, the Korean Catholic Church initiated humanitarian work to assist the refugees, and social activists from all over Korea, dreaming of building Jeju as "the peace island," collaborated effectively, welcoming Yemenese by cultivating a culture of hospitality and by inviting them into their houses. However, few refugees

1. Aschroft et al., *Post-Colonial Studies*, 73.

were accepted by the Korean government, so many people were forced to stay illegally or leave for other countries.

By definition, refugees indicate those who leave their countries due to war, genocide, or natural disaster, and for refugees the most prevailing emotion is fear.[2] After settling down in a new place, they suffer from various physical and/or psychological ills. Originally an international law was drafted after the First World War to protect European exiles who had lost their homes. However, today most refugees are from the Third World, and the number of refugees scattered around the world was sixty-five million in 2016 and is continually increasing.

Some religious communities have responded to the situation by creating living communities with exiled women, and in this way they support women in their adjustment to the new culture as well as provide sisterhood. For example, the Holy Names Sisters invited exiled families into their community and created an intentional living community in Manitoba, Canada. This living community is by nature interreligious and intercultural. Following the model of this Manitoba living community, Delphin Bush, an associate member of the Sisters of Holy Names of Jesus and Mary, created a living community in Portland in collaboration with the SNJM community in 2017. Currently she lives with four exiled women, creating a loving, intentional community.[3] This new style of living community provides a vision for the future, especially given the current ecological and political crises, thus creating many more exiles and refugees. Women religious, then, need to be open and respond creatively to this situation in the spirit of collaboration and networking.

Human Trafficking

Concerning human rights, human trafficking is one of the most shameful problems in today's world. Human trafficking is estimated

2. Smith and Donders, *Refugees Are People*, 3.
3. Grubb, "Mariposa Ministries," para. 1.

to be a $32-billion-a-year global industry. After drug trafficking, human trafficking is the world's second most profitable criminal enterprise. Especially women and young children from Third World countries have been sold as laborers or sex slaves. Women religious in the US, collaborating with the UN and local groups, have actively worked to eradicate this human tragedy, although the effort is still incomplete. Because the victims of trafficking are misplaced to unknown places, they experience severe suffering from alienation and violence, as there is no infrastructure to sustain or protect their human rights.

Trafficking in humans has existed throughout human history (generally in the form of slavery), but contemporary trafficking is more problematic in terms of gender, race, and wealth.[4] Trafficking of women and girls highlights the problems of gender, racism, and poverty around the globe. Most trafficked women come from poor countries of the Global South and are sent to richer countries to earn money for their families or children. In the interviews reported by Human Rights Watch, these women often responded that they needed to do it to support their families.[5] Several women were involved in sex work before they were trafficked because they did not have access to any other job. Also, desperate Third World people who have emigrated illegally seek to improve their living conditions.

Since the IMF crisis of the 1990s, Asian countries have experienced an economic downturn and the problem of unemployment has increased poverty among Asians. In this situation, lots of poor Asian women fall victim to trafficking by unscrupulous business people who gather a cadre of female sex "slaves" for profit. Trafficking in human beings is a crime in which victims are moved from a poor environment to a more affluent one, but the profits flow in the opposite direction. The pattern is often repeated at the domestic, regional, and global levels. The UN Office on Drugs and Crime (UNODC) reported in January 2019 that human trafficking is on

4. United Nations, "Trafficking in Human Beings," para. 7.
5. Varia, "Hidden Victims of Human Trafficking," para. 1.

the rise and more horrific than ever. Also, UNODC mentioned that the global trend has increased steadily since 2010.[6]

Trafficking sometimes involves international marriage and employment as nannies and housemaids, which often results in domestic violence and forced labor. For decades young women from foreign countries such as Vietnam, the Philippines, and Myanmar have married aged Korean farmers. Many foreign brides suffer from loneliness and homesickness as well as sometimes domestic violence. Such international marriage can be counted as immigration, but the whole process is often so violent that it should be considered human trafficking.

The prevention of human trafficking has been very important for women and girls' human rights. In Battayah, Thailand, infamous for its sex industry, religious women support women who are in danger of trafficking. For example, the Good Shepherds Sisters founded the Fountain of Life Women's Center, which provides education and support for vulnerable women who could be easily targeted for human trafficking among the immigrants and refugee who stay in Battayah.[7] Rural areas' poor girls and women are abducted or sold, and many cases remain unreported. However, the danger of being trafficked also exists in the US. Those who are exiles and undocumented immigrants are vulnerable groups being trafficked as well as girls from dysfunctional families and those living in insecure environments.

Women religious in the US and the sisters in the UN particularly work hard to support the survivors of human trafficking in the US, but much more work needs to be done. I believe it is a ministry that requires international collaboration as well as more local and regional collaboration in the area of raising awareness of and education about the serious reality of human trafficking of various forms and the protection of and support for the survivors and the rescued.

---

6. Yakupitiyaga, "Recorded Increase in Human Trafficking," lines 1–6.
7. Fountain of Life Women's Center, "Mission," lines 1–2.

Immigration

Immigration is the other huge global issue that many women religious in the US are actively engaged in. The current problem of immigration comes from the economic structure that creates many immigrants in the US, not necessarily following the American dream but rather simply seeking security. Thus, it is almost impossible to prohibit the flow of human beings. Immigration (both documented and undocumented) signifies a voluntary movement for economic reasons, which creates a diaspora community in the hosting countries, bringing their religions and cultures and resulting in a new multicultural society.

However, this immigrant or diaspora culture does not attain the same power as the mainline culture. These cultures brought by non-European immigrants could be called a subculture, but more specifically subaltern culture, emphasizing the lack of power of the dislocated and the immigrants. Seminal postcolonial scholar Gayatri Spivak analyzed the power difference critically in her work "Can Subaltern Speak?" Spivak describes the subaltern as "bottom layers of society constituted by the specific mode of exclusion from markets, political-legal representation, and the possibility of full membership in a dominant social order."[8] Spivak tells the story of Bhubaneswari Bhaduri, asking why her story could not be heard. Stories such as these underscore that immigration is a human rights matter.

To adjust to a new culture and learn a new language is always challenging, and most immigrants take their voicelessness for granted. Ironically, by emigrating, they also often become strangers in their own lands. Asian American literature describes how eager immigrant families are to visit their countries of origin and how they often do not feel as if they belong when they go there.[9] No matter how painful it was to learn foreign language, these people may no longer speak their mother tongue well. The mother tongue becomes distorted by the other language's accent and distinguishes their

8. Spivak, "Forward," in *A Companion to Postcolonial Studies*, xx.

9. See Tan, *Joy Luck Club*.

speech from that of their fellow countrymen. Their accent again becomes the mark of demarcation. Therefore, many immigrants suffer doubly from alienation and loss of home.

Language or, more biologically speaking, tongue is a metaphor that expresses the discomfort of the dislocated when they learn a new language for survival. In her poem, Therese Hak Kyoung Cha writes:

To bite the tongue.
Swallow. Deep. Deeper.
Swallow. Again even more.
Just until there would be no more or organ
Organ no more.
Cries.

Little at a time. The commas. The periods.
The pauses.
Before and after. Throughout. All advent.
All following.
Sentences.
Paragraphs. Silent. A little nearer. Nearer
Pages and pages
In movement
Line after
Line void to the left void to the right, void the
Words the silences.

I hear the signs. Remnants. Missing.
The mute signs. Never the same.
Absent.[10]

This poem symbolically shows the pain of relocating and of learning the language of the host country. It is a process of losing one's self and of crying. Crying represents being in a state of dislocation. Cha highlights how the dislocated are easily led into being silent, voiceless, and invisible.

As a response to these problems, more women religious in the US are engaging in the current immigration crisis. Some

10. Cha, *Dictee*, 69.

communities support the people who wait for border crossing at the wall, providing food and water; others help those who have just crossed the border with Mexico. For example, the Annunciation House in El Paso, which is run by Loretto sisters, provides a refuge for people who have been released from the detention center. Many other sisters in the US volunteer there as well.[11]

Also, Catholic Charities of the Rio Grande Valley, run by the Missionaries of Jesus, directly supports border-crossing people. Immigration is one of the most striking social justice issues as many uprooted people from Latin American try to cross the border between Mexico and the US.[12] As I mentioned earlier, immigration occurs because of the economic structure and the need for cheap labor, which draws many immigrants. The future of undocumented immigrants, then, has become a pressing human rights issue.

Dislocation, including immigration, is an urgent global problem. With these conditions of immigration, exile, and human trafficking, we experience a multicultural society, and it demands intentional intercultural living.

Remapping the World

We can summarize the world we are living in now as the global capital and cross-cultural world where many people suffer from poverty, dislocation, and invisibility beyond nation, ethnicity, and race. The destructive power of this system worsens the environmental situation, and eco-justice has become a part of the global justice concern. As a response, several socioeconomic theories have emerged aiming at a new perspective of life and at de-globalizing the system. In this section, I will explain the new era of multitude, which can be characterized as digital and global activism and individualism. I will examine two theories of an alternative vision for or against globalization.

11. Becker and Ondreyco, "What It's Like to Accompany Migrants," para. 5.
12. Bourbon, "Moving Beyond the Wall," paras. 7–8.

Era of Multitude

We are living in a new evolving era. Some say that we are living in the fourth industrial revolution. In this era, we have experienced the Arab Spring and many other movements that use the Internet, and social media more specifically, as a way to publish their ideas and communicate them to the world. Regarding this new wave, Antonio Negri, an Italian thinker, calls this the time of *multitude*. The multitude are different from the masses in that the multitude are more individualistic and voluntary subjects. If the masses are messy and often uneducated and need an elite leader, the multitude are those who are educated and have political conscientiousness and act to change the world. In 2018, hundreds of thousands of South Koreans gathered peacefully with candle light asking President Park to resign. Through social media, the movement began and no one could control the widespread participation. All citizens voluntarily engaged and it succeeded. After achieving their goal, the gathering ended automatically.

Another example of a multitude movement is the Occupy Movement seen across the globe today. It manifests a movement where the people as the multitude are aware of inequality in terms of income, with statistics indicating the large gap between the top 1 percent and the global 99 percent. This popular movement demands a decrease in this level of inequality between the rich and the poor.

In this era of the multitude, global activism has become more digitalized, focusing on collaboration and networking. Maybe the religious community should understand the world, then, in terms of digital and global culture in which each individual actively engages in transforming society.

Small Is Beautiful

One of the creative reactions to the global economy that prompts and advocates for mass consumption is the "Small is beautiful" movement. German economic theorist E. Schumacher claimed this slogan "Small is beautiful," which stands in contrast to the current economic system founded on the myth that big is successful and beautiful. Although he talked about sustainability during the energy crisis of the 1970s, the concept is even more applicable today. Simplicity as a value-driven life has become a working force for the eco-justice movement, such as having a small house, which is counter to the American dream, aka Chinese dream.[13]

This theory seems to reveal a new horizon of understanding of human beings and a world with limited sources. He claims that the meaning of freedom and human dignity should be found in a sound economy, which comes from simplicity in terms of lifestyle and sustainability in terms of equal distribution. We witness that the younger generation often intentionally lives as a community in a house as well as in simplicity because of ecological concerns. If we share living space with others, we can save our finite resources.

Furthermore, this idea of "Small is beautiful" helps to make sense of the current situation of religious life. We women religious do not have to consider the diminishing size of our community as a sign of failure, but rather one of a new beginning—more sustainable and open to multiple levels of collaboration with various partners. We will work and live in simplicity, which is one of the fundamental values of the vowed life. In the spirit of simplicity, we can create the freedom to respond to situations promptly.

Delinking Theory

The other approach is delinking theory, which was created by the late Egyptian economist Samir Amin. Amin suggests an alternative system to decolonize the global capitalism. This theory seems to be revitalized now with the Occupy Movement. Amin's theory assumes networking with all Third World countries as well as emerging states that have developed an alternative system, such as China. He argues that the current economic system was established by the imperial powers of the US, Europe, and Japan, and

---

13. See Schumacher, *Small Is Beautiful.*

any alternative system against the given structure was suppressed. In this system, most people fall into poverty, creating a new class system beyond race and nation. As for a better system, he recommends the process of delinking or anti-globalization as a solution to the unequal distribution of wealth in today's world.

In the global capital system, all resources and commodities are linked under the market system. Delinking the monopoly economic system would empower building an alternative anti-monopoly social coalition in the fields of technology, communication, and financial systems. The delinking movement signifies practical action as well as spiritual awareness, creating a conscientious community and constructing global citizenship based on solidarity and human dignity. Although there are many pros and cons regarding delinking theory, a complete reorganization of the world system is a clear need because this socioeconomic system does not include any principle of distribution of resources and products (at present it would be capital or benefit of the capital).

Today, we find remarkable change in that the national borders are becoming porous, and homogeneous cultures do not exist anymore in the world. In the twenty-first-century global and multicultural society, the main culture and the subaltern culture become mixed and create new hybrid cultures. This hybridization includes the ways in which forms become separated from existing practices and recombine with new forms in new practices.[14]

More interestingly, a local culture can become a center too. In other words, the concept of center and margin can be very flexible. For example, in popular culture we enjoy stand-up comedians who carry Palestine, Mexican, Indian, or Vietnamese culture and articulate the reality of multicultural living in the US. Similarly, K-pop music, such as Psy's "Gangnam Style" or BTS' songs such as "Love Yourself" hit the Billboard chart, and the film *Crazy Rich Asians* in 2018 demonstrated an Asian version of a Hollywood film, breaking the stereotypical role of Asian people. Now in social media, Childish Gambino's song "This Is America" hit millions of the views and all global community created parodies of the song such as "This Is

14. Pieterse, *Globalization and Culture*, 231

Nigeria," "This Is Syria," "This Is India," and so on and so forth. As such, they sharply critique the local society.

Also, it is noticeable to see highly educated and high-tech professional immigrants from all over the world as a global phenomenon. They attain a pretty encapsulated luxurious lifestyle as new global aristocrats. In this way of living, poverty does not belong only to minority immigrants. The reality of the global situation is overwhelming, and it is urgent to create a new alternative vision for the world.

Intercultural Living

I find a new road map to reach people and the world where we hear the calling to resist the dominant social order that dehumanizes many people and to create an alternative way of life as women religious in the US and in the global world. As Pope Francis teaches, we are all missionary disciples, and if we cannot live mission, which means leaving our own comfort zone and engaging with others, the community of disciples turns inward and dies.[15] Theologians such as Steve Bevan emphasize mission *toward*, emphasizing the movement of God inside out and the importance of engaging with other cultures and peoples in great humility.[16] As a consequence of our mission in collaboration and networking, it is necessary and natural to live in an intercultural way. In this way, we seek to break all dehumanizing environments that are tightly linked and to build the link of friendship. The space where interculturality occurs is called the liminal space, and I claim that the religious life in the twenty-first century must exist in the interstitial dynamic of diversity, which emphasizes the subversion of the margin and the center, often creating a new hybrid culture.

While being missioned in the world in the twenty-first century, women religious recognize the downsizing of the community, the decrease in religious vocation, and fewer younger sisters

15. Gittins, *Living Mission Interculturally*, 164.
16. Bevans, "God Inside Out," para. 15.

under the age of forty. The decrease of vocation is more a global phenomenon. Countries such as South Korea have experienced an abundance of religious vocation but a decrease in new members. While the vocation from the rural areas of Vietnam still remain high, the cities, such as Ho Chi Minh City, show a decrease of religious vocation. Also, religious communities in South Korea recruit their members from China, Cambodia, and Vietnam, and the first formation becomes multicultural. International congregations such as the Scared Heart have already begun international formation from other countries. In the case of the Giving Voice group, which was composed of sisters under the age of fifty, it has now become smaller. Also, we sense the increase of sisters who are non-Westerners. Due to immigration from the global and multicultural way of life, the religious who have newly joined the community are more diverse in terms of race and ethnicity.

Thus, the necessity becomes intercultural living as a small community, yet effectively connecting one to another. In this network, we would delink any system that negatively affects human dignity, and we would relink with the people who are on the margin so that we build a new alternative way of living as global sisters.

The global living sisterhood of women religious does not necessarily mean a tightly structured community. Rather it signifies a movement or direction toward creativity and interaction, and further development of mission for the people. Actually, intercultural living was originally the missionary orders' concern, but now almost of all of the religious community find an invitation to live interculturally in this multicultural society. Now intercultural living is not simply a theory but a practice, and many people witness that they experience richness and maturity through intercultural living, which challenges us to be free from given cultural structures or religious frames. When women religious live interculturally, the community can be a prophetic sign of harmony and communion in the context of a world wounded by ethnic conflicts and racism.

There is much research on intercultural living as practice. Here, I employ the challenges of intercultural living from the CMF

(Congregatio Missionariorum Filiorum Immaculati Cordis Beatae Mariae Virginis).

Although the description is for an international community, it would be applicable to any form of community that is moving toward intercultural living. The possible challenges and conflicts are as follows:

1. Categorizing the members in terms of ethnicity and race: We easily, whenever we face discomfort, apply prejudice; we tend to point out the member's ethnicity or race, rather than face the concern directly.

2. Cultural domination: In an intercultural community, the predominant group in terms of economic power, race, age, number, and social favors tends to consider themselves as superior and impose their social and cultural norm on the others.

3. Self-victimization: In the intercultural community, those who have low self-esteem perceive certain situations as discrimination or unfair treatment although there are no objective clues.

4. Cultural shield: Some members can use cultural difference for self-defense. When a conflict arises, the members try to excuse their position under the cultural shield.

5. Minority discount: Ethnic minority members can enjoy privileges and acceptance. Without fairness, for example, in the formation community, ethnic minority members' mistakes tend to be easily forgiven.

6. Majority cultural insensitivity: Most often the way to convene the meeting, the choice of language, and the setting of living space follows the culture of the majority group without considering feelings or the comfort level of the minority members.[17]

---

17. I adapted possible conflicts in the intercultural communities from Vattamattam, " Intercultural Living," para. 16.

It is our mission to embody intercultural living as a vocation in the global world of the twenty-first century when demarcating the line between the margin and the center becomes thin.

Now religious life seems to be summoned for the mission in intercultural living. The world is the place where our prophetic vocation is located. As a small group of women, religious women can be friends with many disenfranchised people and this friendship can bring the kingdom of heaven to the *here and now*.

The Jesus Movement

> He said, "Put out into deep water, and let down
> the nets for a catch."
> Simon answered, "Master, we've worked hard
> all night and haven't caught anything.
> But because you say so, I will let down the nets."
>
> —Luke 5:4–5

> "But go, tell his disciples and Peter that he is going
> ahead of you to Galilee;
> there you will see him, just as he told you."
>
> —Mark 16:7

When we talk about the origin of religious life, we talk about desert fathers and mothers, St. Anthony, the first hermit, and Pachomius, the founder of cenobitic monasticism, building the living community of hermits. In terms of the rules and the life of solitude and prayer, it is appropriate to consider this tradition as the origin of religious life. It is also true that religious life has often been equivalent to cloistered life or monasticism. We learned that the first Western monastic tradition came from Benedictine abbey, and it has had a great influence on religious life by emphasizing stability.

However, the apostolic religious life, emerging from the mission and calling in the world as dwellers in the liminal space, finds the origin alternately. This movement, which is deeply related to apostolic religious women, is the *apotactic movement*. Those involved in the *apotactic* movement were often referred to as the village ascetics, and they adopted a life of simplicity and celibacy, creating small cluster groups in towns and cities in Syria and Palestine.[1] They resided in the liminal space between the secular and the sacred. The first apotactics were the sacred virgins throughout the second and the third centuries. By opting for the virginal state, they lived singly and met frequently together in their homes for dialogue and prayer. The life of virgins who wanted not to marry but to live alone or together with other women and seek religious devotion in the midst of normal urban life[2] would be an exemplary case of living in the liminal space as the prototype of religious women in *apostolica*. Scholar of religious life Sandra Schneiders claims the virgin movement signified women's resistance against the empire and family life, which assigned them a role of submission and reproduction.[3]

Along with this historical linking of the women's movement of apostolic freedom, foregrounding the mission and service of the gospel value in the global world as dwellers in the liminal space, I find deep roots of the apostolic religious life in the Jesus movement. These roots spring from Jesus as the border-crosser who frequently crossed the boundaries of Gentiles and Jews, and from the disciples, who continued Jesus' proclamation that the kingdom of heaven was near in the light of resurrection. It is also crucial to understand the Jesus movement as ongoing. I will describe the Jesus movement as an interpretation beginning with the return to Galilee, and there are three elements to the interpretation of the Jesus movement.

Returning to Galilee

Whenever I listen to the vocation stories of women religious, I recognize that their experience of calling is deeply rooted in a personal relationship with Jesus. No matter what kind of ministry they are involved in or what kind of theology they embrace,

1. Goehring, *Ascetics, Society and Desert,* 26.
2. McNamara, *Sisters in Arms,* 38.
3. O'Murchu, *Religious Life in the 21ˢᵗ Century,* 71–72.

religious life is fundamentally given by the calling of Jesus. Thus, when I hear that an individual stands in uncertainty in terms of their vocation of religious life and ministry, I suggest we go back to the space that we call Galilee.

Galilee is a symbolic space in which the two dimensions of chronology and geography coexist. In this liminal space, women religious can regain a vitality of mission. In the Gospel of Mark's resurrection narrative, the angel says to the women who visit Jesus' tomb, "But go, tell his disciples and Peter that he is going ahead of you to Galilee; there you will see him" (16:7). Interestingly, the narrative of the gospel says that the women could not say anything because of fear. When even the women in the story, who followed Jesus until his death and sought him even in the empty tomb, were terrified, the narrative does not say whether the women got over their fear or if they went to Galilee with the male disciples. It seems easier to be frozen and stuck in a traumatic situation. However, the message is very clear: they should go back to Galilee and there they will retell their vocation and life in a new way. At least from the perspective of Mark's Gospel, the Jesus movement, which followed an understanding of the meaning of resurrection, coincides with a return to Galilee.

In one's personal journey, a person easily recognizes the concentric circle that begins at Galilee and returns to Galilee. In the spring day that began the mission and vocation, women religious were fostered by Jesus in Galilee, no matter their location. Galilee could be Seoul, Rome, or any small town in the Global South. It could be a moment of meditation or any "Aha!" moment when a person recognizes their passion, ministry, and calling through intimacy with Jesus.

In Galilee, many women religious have grasped various moments of mystical union with Jesus. Depending on her spiritual and psychological development, she could see Jesus as her lover, companion, teacher, mother, or father. Through this period, she can recognize her inner wounds, hurt, and misplaced passion for Jesus (if indeed she carried these), as well as find her hope. If there is anyone who wants to go back to Galilee, one of the most life-giving statements from the Gospel of Mark is that Jesus will meet her there. Most women religious say that they bring their own sense of confusion and frustration that comes from uncertainty about religious life.

The cycle of returning to Galilee is applicable to religious life in general. In the midst of frustration and uncertainty, women religious as a group are invited to this cycle, which is organically connected with the Jesus movement. The earthly Jesus began his mission in Galilee, where he called his disciples; from there, he continuously sent out his disciples to the world (Matthew 10; Mark 6; Luke 9–10). After confirming the identity of Jesus as Messiah, they went to Jerusalem and experienced failure and trauma through the death of Jesus on the Cross. There they stood on the thin borderland where they neither belonged to the world nor to Jesus. They lost their direction, but there the disciples heard that they should return to Galilee. After their exciting mission under the guidance of Jesus, they lost the vision of the messianic hope. The only thing they could cling to was companionship with other disciples until they had the confidence for the future. In that companionship, they would meet Jesus again even though they did not understand what it meant. Paradoxically, it marked the beginning of the Jesus movement in trust and hope for the future.

The Jesus Movement

What is the Jesus movement? The Jesus movement occurred after Jesus' death. It is obvious the disciples were scattered yet regathered in the spirit of the resurrection.[4] The kingdom of heaven, which was proclaimed by Jesus, did not arrive immediately, and we do not know what happened to the disciples. Scholars such as Michael White argue that the first Jesus movement was a small Jewish sectarian group.[5] I understand the Jesus movement in the light of

---

4. Elizondo, *Galilean Journey*, 79
5. White, "Jesus Movement," para. 3.

the Gospel of Mark,[6] which is the earliest text, predating the other two Synoptic Gospels, to say nothing of the distinct Gospel of John, which seems to have been written as late as A.D. 100. Once the disciples returned to Galilee, they understood themselves, the world, and God in light of the resurrection.

The Jesus movement is the actualization of Jesus' vision and life in the light of the resurrection through remembering and interpreting the Jesus event. The Jesus event can be summarized as Jesus, the Son of God, proclaiming that the kingdom of heaven is here and now or at least near. The resurrected Jesus commanded his disciples to go into the world proclaiming the good news. Here, the world they went back to is represented as Galilee, where they met Jesus and worked with him continuously in the vision of the kingdom of God.

The Jesus movement was to revitalize Judean religion through returning to God's heart and restoring the right relationship. Jesus set up the sacrament of friendship, which is open to everybody and which creates an egalitarian community.

Through the history of Christianity, there have been many groups who revitalized the Jesus movement. During the medieval period, we recognize women struggling to attain the freedom to serve the poor as a way of following the Jesus movement. For example, St. Clare, who was inspired by the Franciscan movement, pursued the apostolic freedom to go and serve the poor. Obviously, during the thirteenth century many women wanted to be part of the apostolic community. However, the church proclaimed that women religious should be cloistered, and St. Clare struggled against the institutional church.[7] During this time, the third order and the Beguines functioned as apostolic agents to serve the poor. For example, St. Catherine of Siena served the poor as a third-order Dominican. The third order was a group of people who lived in a liminal way. As a part of a particular religious community, the members of the third order followed the rule of the community

6. The Gospel of Mark is considered to have been written around 60 CE, Matthew around 70–80, and Luke around 80–90.

7. Park, "St. Clare."

and functioned as members of the community, yet they were not the same as the religious members who lived cloistered communal lives. In a similar vein, in the late medieval period of Europe, the Beguines engaged with the poor in the world through their service and work while they studied and preached the gospel. In these ways, women actively engaged in the Jesus movement, a movement that is always new and moving.

An Interpretation of the Jesus Movement

The Jesus movement has continued until now. According to the time and place, the Jesus movement has been interpreted and actualized. For today's world, we women religious need to actualize the Jesus movement through an interpretation that exists in a dialectical dynamic between explanation and understanding.[8] Understanding indicates the process of making sense through grasping and a critique of the explanation of the Jesus movement. Through this process, we reach the point of appropriation or application to the religious life, which leads to transformation. The interpretation of the Jesus movement includes three elements: to embrace intimacy with Jesus, to understand the Jesus movement as process, and to appropriate the Jesus movement.

To Embrace Intimacy with Jesus

The Jesus movement begins with intimacy with Jesus and in an action of interpretation, the intimacy with Jesus brings an essential aspect of affection. Jesus called his disciples by speaking the simple words, "Follow me" (Mark 1:17; 2:14; John 1:43). The word *disciple* comes from the Latin *discipulus*, meaning "learner." In this case, learning is not just an intellectual process of gaining knowledge but rather one of attaining a more embodied knowledge. In this learning process, a disciple becomes a follower, one who trusts and believes in a teacher and learns the master's words and example. It

8. Schneiders, *Revelatory Text*, 159–61.

is essential for a disciple to enter into an intimate, instructive, and imitative relationship with the master. Thus, we can see that this intimate relationship creates a space for a disciple to *discipline* herself in terms of her life commitment as a woman religious.

Furthermore, the intimate relationship with Jesus develops as friendship. Jesus calls his disciples friends, not servants (John 15:15). Among those things prized in the Greco-Roman world was friendship, and this required mutual serviceability and affection.[9] In the ancient time, to be a friend with someone was to share one's life or destiny.[10] In Confucian culture, friendship is one of the foundational principles of society, and it requires faithfulness. In friendship, one has the obligation to take a friend's role as the householder or family member when the friend is absent.

As an interpretation of the Jesus movement, intimacy with Jesus brings the aspect of affection and mutuality. Applying the intimacy with Jesus to the community of women religious, we can turn to the affectionate stories of our founders with Jesus. Most often, the founding community was strong and passionate, yet small and vulnerable. As a new beginning in the Jesus movement, the new disciples went back to Galilee, where they met Jesus and learned how to be Jesus' companions.

Women religious, as congregations, should then go back to the Galilee where they began to fall in love with Jesus. Then, as the disciples reunderstand their life and vocation, women religious as communities need to reappreciate their religious life in community now. To return to Galilee symbolizes going back to the beginner's mind and embracing the second naiveté that emphasizes dreaming again the mission of the community in the spirit of friendship with Jesus on a personal level. This can result in refoundation or completion or anything else on the congregational level. However, it is not our task to figure that out but to seek what is coming in terms of intimacy and love. In intimacy with Jesus, women religious taste emotions, memories, and an unexpected vision. The friendship that

9. Meilander, "Friendship in the Classical World," para. 7.
10. Schneiders, *Written That You May Believe*, 172.

emphasizes their mutual affection is an everlasting light and guide in the Jesus movement as an art of interpretation.

To Understand the Jesus Movement as Process

If we want to approach the Jesus movement as an art of interpretation, it is crucial to understand it as an ongoing process, not a set of tasks. As a mechanism of interpretation, we consider the dialectical dynamic between explanation and understanding. Eventually, we reach a point where we can create meaning, which means we fully understand the significance of the text. In this case, the text could be a written text as well as a gesture, movement, or body, including the body of an institution. Interpretation includes particularity as an input for interpretation, and appropriation as an application to the situation. This process should be located in a cycle that increases in depth through time.

For example, if we interpret the Jesus movement in the current religious life in the US, there will be process or change according to the interpreter's position in the cycle, and through investigation of the cycle we can project the direction where we are heading. This process moves between the two poles of explanation and understanding. In this process, we can add questions and doubts as well as give general understanding. Once we acquire intimacy with Jesus, we can expel fear or anxiety in the process of interpretation.

In this hermeneutical cycle of the Jesus movement, there arise numerous questions because the answers given are only partially satisfactory and raise more questions. For example, we can bring the questions about the three vows: Is it still meaningful to keep these vows? Is it possible to dialogue about the three vows with others who are not accustomed to religious life? And is there any possibility to explore new names or new interpretations of the vows? Another case could be about community life: What does it mean to live in community as members of an apostolic community? Is community living limited to living in the same house? And so on and so forth. A series of questions will search for explanations.

If we apply the Jesus Movement as an interpretation, we should be consistent and honest. Because the interpretation process is ongoing, the meaning that is created through the interpretation is always temporary. Thus, the virtue of this movement lies in religious women as individuals or as community consistently needing to be attuned to the movement in the spirit of discernment. Along with consistency, honesty is a crucial element in this process to create meanings that guide us into new ways of religious life. Free from any entitlement or pressure, anyone who interprets the Jesus Movement as the source of religious life will have the inner strength to face frustration and confusion as well as loneliness and alienation.

Perhaps Galilee is metaphorical space where women religious as individuals or institutions feel security in the midst of intimacy with Jesus and engage honestly in interpretation as a process. Just as the first disciples reached the final stage of appropriation in terms of interpretation of the Jesus Movement, although we cannot know how they reached that point, we should be included in this process.

To Appropriate the Jesus Movement

The goal of interpretation is to reach the point of appropriation, which strongly suggests that the created meaning will be employed to transform the life of the subjects of interpretation. Here the acquired meaning is not epistemological knowledge but an ontological one that involves the totality of being human. When the dialectic between explanation and understanding has been achieved, the mind comes to rest in understanding, that is, in the experience of meaning. Also, more importantly, it involves engagement with the text, and the Jesus Movement in particular as interpretation.

What does it mean to appropriate the Jesus Movement? It means to adopt the new meaning that emerged from the interpretation into the religious life for today. Appropriation is the term indicating that the interpreters are engaged with the process wherein the readers make their own cultural meanings.[11] In other words, in this transformative moment, we as women religious fully embody the meaning of the Jesus Movement in our own context, which can be summarized as follows: 1) the global capitalistic world system in which many people suffer from lack of resources, 2) religious vocations becoming smaller and smaller and becoming a position of the minority, and 3) many alternative ways to construct a more just world.

Thus, we can say that the Jesus Movement itself was very particular in the context of the first century, as led by Jesus, who proclaimed that the kingdom of heaven was near. The movement was appropriated by the first disciples, who felt lost when they experienced the death of their master. Through the process of interpretation of the resurrection in Galilee, they understood their new identity and new mission. Similar to being in the terrain of Galilee, we are in the process of interpretation of the Jesus Movement that emphasizes the human experience in our global world and in our mission. Thus, in the appropriation, we should emphasize the notion of intercultural living, mobility, and global networking as well as a new understanding of religious life.

11. Young, *Formation of Christian Culture*, 9. See also Lee, "Bible in Chinese Christianity."

Vows: Living in the Liminal Space

It's the heart afraid of breaking, that never learns to dance,
It's the dream afraid of waking, that never takes the chance,
It's the one who won't be taking, who cannot seem to give,
And the soul afraid of dying, that never learns to live,

—"Rose" by Amanda McBroom

There is no doubt that vows express the meaning of religious life, and due to their importance, there are ample resources to explain this meaning. Nevertheless, the written documents do not seem to articulate well the current lived experiences. The writings on the three vows are not wrong per se, but we feel a new language is required to communicate with a world that is multicultural, global, and interreligious. In my religious studies classes, I experience frustration when explaining the vows to my students. It is astonishing to realize that we have used the same language with those who know about religious life. We assume that everybody understands religious vows in the Catholic Church. Now we need to use the same language of the new generation of the so-called "nones," who neither understand religious life nor have any direct relationships with women religious. This chapter explores new languages of vows.

A New Language of Vows

A missionary sister said, "I learned the indigenous language and tried a dialogue with the elder of the tribe. After my talk, the elder looked at me and said that I definitely use their language, yet the elder does not understand me at all." Often, we communicate with people without considering their perceptions.

In this secularized world, we face the reality that most college students have little knowledge of the Christian faith, even when they attend Catholic colleges. The language of our vows is far from our daily experience as women religious. Alternatively, our lifestyle, which has been elaborated in the discourses of religious life, seems to have little or no connection to the lives of young people.

In a similar vein, a friend in Korea who lives as a consecrated virgin cautiously asked, "Um, what do you think of the concept of consecrated virgins? I have lived happily as one, but when young women ask me what the meaning of my virginity is, I do not know how to explain . . ." In this new emerging secular world, with which we want to engage deeply, how can we communicate with people—young people in particular—about vows or the vowed life? We believe it is time to sing a new song to the Lord (Psalm 96:1) and to the world, by creating new hymns and melodies.

When the language—in the case of the narrative of our vowed life—is restricted by grammar, programmed by the documents of the church, and just mindlessly repeated, its vivid meanings will die out, sooner or later. As psychoanalyst Jacques Lacan says, we are spoken rather than speaking. We are conditioned by the given paradigm and structure in our thinking and speech. But we must acknowledge that it is impossible to completely leave behind the language that describes religious life since it is still beneficial for constructing a meaning for vowed life and is the language we have used throughout ongoing formation. Now, however, considering religious life as life in liminal space, we can try to create a new language as an expression of our lived experience and in so doing enrich the meaning of religious life in today's world.

Regarding new language, Mexican American feminist Gloria Anzaldúa talks about the possibility of a new language emerging from the experience of the dwellers of liminal space. Anzaldúa poetically explains that "Chicano Spanish is not incorrect; it is a living language." She further asks, "For a people who are neither Spanish nor live in a country in which Spanish is the first language; for a people who live in a country in which English is the reigning tongue but who are not Anglo; for a people who cannot entirely identify with either standard Spanish nor standard English, what recourse is left to them but to create their own language?"[1]

We women religious of the twenty-first century live in a global world where many cultural elements collide in fusion or hybridity. Yet our *unique* charism and the call from the spirit of Christ, which is beyond cultural phenomena, should stand firm. Thus, any new language should be grounded in a matter of the divine and human simultaneously, so that we can effectively strengthen and increase the body of Christ.[2]

A danger within vowed life is avoiding sharing stories about the personal experiences of the vows. Whether these stories are about growing older or discerning ministries or the frustration of living a prophetic vocation in the community, they can reveal and reflect on the lived experiences of vows. In that sense, telling stories is an epistemology on religious life. We find that the personal stories of women religious and their communities are not spoken of by the women themselves, but are rather spoken of by a few theologians or academic women religious.

A lack of narrative does not mean women religious have quit the mission, along with presence and prayer ministry in contemplation. The lack is merely due to the aging of women religious—and perhaps a sense of failure and shame in the culture, which admires youth and productivity. Women religious rather tend to talk more about the values and struggles of vows in a spiritual direction or other more personal settings than public ones. Lacking discourse means no shared vision or common understanding of the vows. Therefore, in order to lift the rejuvenating values of vowed life, we need to listen to these stories. Perhaps the stories may be full of confusion, doubt, and uncertainty, which are very characteristic of liminal space. But the stories can finally lead to a shared vision and an emergence of a new understanding of religious life in the twenty-first century. This could be the paradigm shift in which each

1. Anzaldúa, *Borderlands La Frontera*, 77.
2. *Perfectae Caritas*, 617.

sister can bring her own experience and then create a new story together. This chapter is an effort to create a new story, to fit with the
new paradigm of religious life as liminal space as well as to apply to
the current reality of globalization.

It is clear that the word *vow* signifies the solemn promise
to God within a particular community. The vows ceremony is
one of the most joyful events of community life. Members of the
community mark a new phase of their journey of religious life
with the vowing member(s), and in this multicultural milieu,
recently joined younger sisters bring their cultural heritage or
unique personal expressions of their commitment to their community's vow ceremony.

Also, the action of making vows has a public dimension so
that it functions as a witness of the charism of religious life, which
stands counterculturally in many aspects. Monastic communities
confess four vows: obedience, poverty, chastity, and residence; while
most apostolic women religious confess three vows of chastity,
obedience, and poverty. Chastity, obedience, and poverty challenge
human desire in general, and this negation exists as a prophetic
action to indicate the transcendental value of the human being.
Due to this act of making vows, women religious around the globe
feel connected to one another. Sr. Sarah Kohls mentions how vows
fascinate her because they bind her to her community members as
well as women religious everywhere, though the precise words we
all say differ.[3] As a unifying force among women religious, vows
shed light on the very understanding of religious life.

Myths of Vows

Before we look at the meaning of vows, we would like to address
the myths of vows. In other words, we will clarify what is not
our approach to religious vows. At least currently, we would say
some approaches to the vowed life do not match the present or
emerging religious life.

3. Kohls, "Something Old, Something New," 17.

One of the most common myths of vows is that they are *a set of rules*. Vows have functioned as a juridical standard, and the vowed life has connoted a way to escape from a world that is sinful and alluring, even among apostolic women religious whose calling is to serve the world. In 313, the Roman Emperor Constantine accepted Christianity and people who dreamed of martyrdom ran away from the world and pursued alternative ways of being martyrs. This ethos of separating oneself from the city influenced the understanding of vows. To be passive, submissive, and aloof is considered holy (or at least desirable) among sisters, and this understanding is not different from expectations of women in general.

In the case of women religious in Asian countries, which have strong Buddhist traditions, this tendency is more robust. Non-attachment is more strongly required than a passion for the world. My first formation in Korea caused a strong sense of confusion because the language of formation was very much like the Buddhists' virtues of detachment or even hatred of the world.

In general, we tend to understand vowed life as the ascetic life, which is inclined toward abstention, rejection, and self-denial. Asceticism itself is not bad, and religious life—as a way to be whole by serving the world—should accept this dimension of negation. Nevertheless, it is obvious that religious life is not just about achieving holiness through a negation of the world. In the fourth century, desert monasteries or desert fathers and mothers who had "left the world" still served people by providing hospitality and wise consultations. Furthermore, the desert community was deeply engaged in helping peasants who were fighting against the high taxation of the Roman Empire.[4] As such, the nature of the vow of negation could be reconsidered and rewritten.

In this regard, the vow of chastity does not merely mean not having sex. It includes the full development of the human person and involves rich relationships with many people. In a way, a vow, as an expression of religious life, should be emphasized as embracing, collaborating with, and serving the world, while not being absorbed into the world.

4. Miller, "Understanding Desert Monasticism," para. 9.

John's Gospel shows two different understandings of the world (cosmos). While the Gospel says, "The God loved the world so much he gave his only Son" (3:16), the same Gospel argues in 15:18–19 that "if you belonged to the world, it would love you as its own. As it is, you do not belong to the world, but I have chosen you out of the world. That is why the world hates you." In this sense, one's attitude toward the world exists in the line in-between two different directions; the vow of religious life, then, exists in the liminal space.

The other common myth of vows is that they are a closed canon of rules rather than an orientation with much space for interpretation. In our traditional approach, vows are considered strict, rather than something offering growth and openness. When we understand a vow as the rule of law and a duty that we must adhere to perfectly, the vowed life can become very legalistic and even punitive.

One of the fundamental dangers of this understanding of vows is legalism. In this narrow approach of vows as a set of rules, women religious easily become judgmental and violent. When we become judgmental of ourselves, we are easily frustrated and guilt-ridden. When we become judgmental of others, we are jealous and oppressive, in the name of the vows. If we make any mistakes or offenses, it can bring a sense of shame or even dismissal from the community.

Are there any alternative ways to understand vows? Diarmuid O'Murchu suggests using the word *for* rather than *of* as a way to avoid characterizing vows as a clear-cut guideline for living in definiteness. Vows should be comprehended as a process to be activated, denoting movement, action, growth, change, and possibility.[5] In this way, O'Murchu invites us to create a space for creativity, exploration, and an expansion of the understanding of vows from just a set of rules. Thus, we need to listen carefully to our stories of embodied experiences of vowed life, so as to interpret them in a new way, which will fit our experiences of ministry and identity.

5. O'Murchu, *Poverty, Celibacy, and Obedience*, 29.

An Alternative View on Vows

If we wish to consider vows as the movement to create a space for renovation and creativity—in order to promote the Jesus movement, which emphasizes the kingdom of God *here and now*—we must examine some concepts of vows.

Vows as Covenant

One way to explain the vow is through covenant. Although this way of explaining the vow has negative aspects, it will bring out the affectionate aspect of the vowed life. In the Hebrew Scriptures, Israel and God made a covenant so that Israel would be faithful and God would protect Israel. This kind of covenant comes from the ancient Suzerain law, which presupposes an unequal power between the two parties involved in the contract. Israel, by nature, would be imperfect or unable to fulfill the promise. Likely, when we women religious approach the three vows as a covenant with God, we tend to carry the burden of perfection, which inevitably results in frustration and even guilt from not being able to complete our contract. During our novitiate, we still remember our chapter on every Friday, when we confessed our guilt over such things as breaking plates or being late to a prayer meeting. The more we desire to be perfect, the more guilt we feel by the very nature of the covenant. Very often, women religious dream of being excellent and perfect, but most of the college students Sophia interviewed wanted to work with sisters who seemed more natural and ordinary, not heroic.[6]

In carefully examining the true meaning of the covenant with God, we find that it is not to be perfect and excel in everything, but to embody and actualize the heart of God, *hessed*, which means compassion. In the book of Hosea, God pleads for Israel to understand the heart of God (2:22). It is clear that the covenantal relationship will manifest in seeking justice out of love for God and for the world.

6. There was a small survey done among the college students of Holy Names University that asked what kind of sisters are ideal partners to work with. I list their responses as an appendix.

Seeking justice can be summarized as seeking a righteous relationship. The commandments that Moses received from God on the mountain of Horeb show two dimensions of a righteous relationship: a righteous relationship with God, and a righteous relationship with other people. The first three commandments indicate how to make a righteous relationship with God, and the rest indicate a righteous relationship with people, and these two aspects are interrelated, not separated. Then, the vow as covenant is an invitation to walk into a righteous relationship to demonstrate an action for love and justice. The pursuit of love and justice will then find expression in the vowed life of chastity, poverty, and obedience.

Of importance is that the covenantal relationship begins with a call by God. The first covenant in the Hebrew Scriptures shows that it was Yahweh who initiated the relationship and the counterpart then engaged. When Jesus created the sacrament of friendship at the Last Supper, he initiated by inviting his beloved disciples, which the Mass canon beautifully elaborates: Jesus called his disciples whom he loved.

Vows as Wisdom

We can understand the vows as Wisdom. In the Hebrew scriptures, we find an elaboration of the nature of Wisdom:

> There is in her a spirit that is intelligent, holy,
> unique, manifold, subtle,
> mobile, clear, unpolluted,
> distinct, invulnerable, loving the good, keen,
> irresistible, beneficent, humane,
> steadfast, sure, free from anxiety,
> all-powerful, overseeing all,
> moreover, penetrating through all spirits
> that are intelligent, pure, and altogether subtle.
>
> For wisdom is more mobile than any motion;
> because of her pureness, she pervades and penetrates all
> things. (Wisdom 7:22–24)

In this view from Scripture, the vows are a life orientation that begins with God's calling and culminates with ministry in the world through the central tendency toward love and justice. When we reflect on this passage on Wisdom, we are struck by her humaneness because we have often perceived the vowed life as being heroic, driven to excellence and perfection, and possibly violent toward human nature. According to the nature of Wisdom, the vowed life should be mobile, which means being flexible, adaptable, and open.

The nature of flexibility originates from a sense of freedom that one's opinion or conviction does not fulfill all aspects of truth and shows a readiness to learn from others. The beauty of adaptability presumes that all things are on the move and communicating always with others, not insisting on positions or presuppositions. This openness represents the humility that we need to learn all the time. In Korea, when a person dies, they call him or her "a student of life," and this appellation strongly carries the Confucian value of learning. The soul is a person who has completed one's journey of life as a studious learner. We believe every woman religious is a student learning the mystery of God through encountering the world on the life journey.

A similar concept to Wisdom could be *Tao*, which is translated into English as "the Way." The most well-known book of Taoism is *Tao Te Ching* by Lao Tzu. The first passage of *Tao Te Ching* describes the nature of Tao, using the image of water, as follows:

> The great Tao is like a flood
>
> It can flow to the left or the right
> The myriad things depend on it for life, but it never stops
>
> It achieves its work but does not take credit
> It clothes and feeds myriad things, but does not rule over them.
> (34.1–5)[7]

The vows as the Way (Tao) could be a gentle expression of the lives of women religious who go anywhere to serve in joy, freedom,

---

7. Lao Tzu, *Tao Te Ching*, para. 34.

and the power that comes from gospel values. We feel, in this approach, that vowed life could remain the very essence of feminine strength. The vowed life can also function as a shared value among sisters, rather than as a coercive system. This shared value would be a gentle and persistent commitment to seek justice and love in the light of the gospel value that emerges from Christ. Thus, vows are not a set of boundaries cast in permanent legal structures, but are a set of spiritual commitments that requires a creative and open-ended engagement and exploration.[8]

With vows as an expression of the shared value that we need to constantly engage with and explore, according to the context, we need to reconsider their meaning in light of consecrated life. The word *consecrated* emphasizes the notion of "setting apart" for the service of God.[9] However, this approach is incomplete. The meaning of consecrated life should highlight the aspect of being *within* the world. In other words, women religious are set apart to exist *in* the world as agents of the kingdom of heaven.

Today, we see men and women in other religions that serve the world. Alternatively, we see social workers who dedicate their careers to serve the disadvantaged and the poor. They do their charity work and commit to social justice. Our only differences come from the vows we take, which are expressions of a profound unity with Jesus as a part of the Jesus movement and a commitment to gospel values in the world. From the source of religious vocation, some women religious serve as professional educators, social workers, activists, and community builders.

The Three Vows

The three vows are embodied expressions of religious life in the world, as well as a life orientation to lead and guide us to be whole. The three vows of chastity, obedience, and poverty are profoundly interconnected and emerge from the commitment to gospel values

8. O'Murchu, *Poverty, Celibacy, and Obedience*, 33.
9. *Perfectae Caritas*, 612.

and a deep sense of freedom. The vows indicate that we are headed freely to the kingdom of heaven and guide us to deepen Jesus' values, which are countercultural. In so doing, they indicate the transcendental aspect of life. The vowed life and the vows exist to promote our mission in an integrated way.

Chastity

In today's society, one major stumbling block to religious life is the vow of chastity. The way of chastity remains a life of being open to God as a disciple of Jesus or a member of the Jesus movement. Chastity includes celibacy, which means voluntary singlehood, refraining from marriage, and living in a religious community. It is not directly related to virginity, nor does it suggest being an asexual being. Ironically, the goal of chastity is to grow into full humanity and does not necessarily exclude the sexual dimension. In the nineteenth century, many religious communities directly or indirectly expected prospective members to be virgins, and many devotions are deeply related to the Virgin Mary.

When we have dialogues with young people about religious life, some of them still ask whether sisters must be virgins. However, we know that virginity is an indication that young women have the vigor and power to give life; it is not necessarily about the virginity itself.[10] The fact that the word *virgin* has strong connections with virginity itself seems to be related to our patriarchal culture, which enforces women's virginity as a way to maintain our subservient position.

Our understanding of the sexual dimension is considered so personal that we do not openly talk about chastity. Instead, there is a tendency to go to psychotherapy or spiritual direction to do so. We cannot change the current culture, but at least we must mention it explicitly, and confront its direction and limits. Women religious went through a very brave exploration period of their sexuality during and after the Second Vatican Council. They sincerely examined

10.

who they were sexually and responded honestly and, because of this, many young women left their communities.

We believe this spirit should continue and encourage women religious to explore and, as a consequence, become themselves. Thus, the way of chastity will not be stagnant, but become a loving dynamic with which they can be free to serve the world entirely and joyfully. For that, we need a sense of freedom to experiment and to make mistakes. Without trials and errors, it is quite impossible to reach one's unique way of being chaste.

As we mentioned earlier, a single being does not mean an asexual being. According to Origen, God is *eros*, who represents connecting and communicating energy. The human being as *Imago Dei* shares God's attribute of *eros*. For the full development of humanity, we need to be sexual beings with *eros*, which helps people to connect and have compassion for those who suffer, especially with the vow of chastity without self-knowledge or a general understanding of human development of sexual and psychological dimensions. Also, the spirit of connectedness should extend to a relationship with nature and all living things. The ground, water, air, and every living thing in the world should participate in our circle of intimacy and relationship.

The vow of chastity challenges our current culture. Most young people live together without marriage, and it is challenging to find people who think that sex is only for procreation. Lifelong commitments seem almost impossible, given the high rate of divorce, and countless people suffer from severe loneliness. The vow of chastity embraces human nature as relational, but not specifically engaged with anyone. Nevertheless, for women religious, the commitment to love people and the world is permanent.

The vow of chastity signifies freedom from gender division. In our spirit of chastity, we can create the freedom of gender norms, which are deeply missing in patriarchy. Many young students claim that they want to work with sisters who do not have any judgments against LGBT people.[11] It is unclear how many genders exist in contemporary society, but it is certainly more

11. See the appendix.

than two, including gender non-conforming, which is an umbrella term indicating anyone who does not feel comfortable with the gender given at birth.[12] The vow of chastity can create a space to include anyone because it exists beyond gender by negating any gender specificity.

It is crucial to understand that gender is not a biological term but rather a social construct. In a way, gender has functioned as a tool to sustain social order and has often been used to oppress women and other sexual minorities. By embracing a variety of genders, women religious—through the vow of chastity—can negate any prejudices and judgments based on gender. This approach can empower many people who struggle with their gender.

The meaning of chastity indicates a specific type of friendship with anyone, not sexually engaged but humanely standing for the person, and in so doing we can fight against human alienation. So, the vow of chastity is the vow of friendship. As Jesus calls his disciples *friends*, a friendship can be open to all people of any gender, race, or class.

Liminal space exists as an in-betweenness, which means we do not situate ourselves at any particular position but *hold open gently*, because of uncertainty. Religious communities would apply these principles to their members also. Inside the communities, if members could explore their gender or sexual orientation freely, in the spirit of celibacy and without judgment, then the community can become open dialogue partners.

In the discourse of religious life, the meaning of intimacy has been ambiguous. Primarily, in American culture, the word *intimacy* connotes a sexual relationship. In Asian cultures, people are more used to emotional and spiritual intimacy. Confucius's teachings emphasize the value of friendship. One of the leading teachings of Confucius is that friends should be faithful. The concern is not whether or not one should have intimate friends, but that one retains inner freedom in intimate relationships. A mature religious should maintain a level of intimacy that keeps her integrity, and the whole community should support her, based on trust and respect.

12 "How Many Genders Are There?," para. 3.

An older sister confessed at a retreat, "I broke my vow of chastity; I was not content in loneliness and felt grumpy." She was honest and humble in that she showed a deep level of integrity. Like the other two vows, the vow of chastity should make us a more genuine and vulnerable human beings.

In acknowledging the pain of clerical sexual abuse against women and children, women religious should stand up and voice the experiences of their own sexual abuse. It would be a loving act of solidarity with all people who have undergone this hardship, and a prophetic action of justice that asks for a righteous relationship with male authority in the church.[13]

The vow of chastity requires bold honesty. We hear the unusual story of the desert mother Sarah, who sat by the water for twenty years, wanting to eradicate her sexual and carnal desires. This story is remarkable because she was very honest with herself and others, and she was very healthy in that she claimed her sexual desire. In feminist discourse, we often hear that women do not express their sexual desire; only men express it. In this case, the *amma* Sarah, as the leader and a woman, boldly reveals her vulnerable yet pure energy, not hiding her carnal or unintegrated desire. In this twenty-first century, we still need her bold and honest spirit.

How can the vow of chastity of friendship be applied to our current world? The apostolic religious life is founded on the spirit of mission, which requires freedom to go whenever and wherever. As Abraham left, at the age of seventy, for the land that God was to show (did not show), women religious who confess the vow of chastity have the freedom to leave anytime for mission, rather than remaining in a comfortable convent or apartment.

In this global age, the vow of chastity can appear to be a desire to listen to God's calling and to have the freedom to leave. Perhaps, in the global market system, we—with our freedom to go anywhere, like flowing water—can *delink* the monopoly system

13. Recently, the general superior of women religious recommended that women religious who have experienced clerical sexual abuse report it and that their communities support those sisters. The "Me Too" movement among women religious will bring a mature understanding of the vow of chastity.

that oppresses so many people around the world.[14] Moreover, we can *relink* with sisters and brothers in the spirit of friendship. If we hear the cry of people in Asia or Africa, we should go and find allies to work with and create a new network of friendship. This would be a great fruit of the vow of chastity.

In conclusion, the meaning of chastity is friendship, and as such we can fight against human alienation. So, the vow of chastity is the vow of friendship. As Jesus calls his disciples friends, they can make friends with people of all genders, races, and classes. Without any attached relationships, women religious can go anywhere in the global world. The vow of chastity, as a lifestyle, can provide the freedom to work with anyone who wants to collaborate within the spirit of connection. This freedom and liberation will bring a deep sense of joy to women religious, as well as to their world.

Poverty

We live in a consumer society where people feel valued when they possess resources. Notably, in today's capital global system, almost everyone desires to have more, but ironically many people fall into poverty. The disparity between the rich and the poor is a serious problem. So what is the meaning of the vow of poverty?

The vow of poverty should also be interpreted differently according to the times. For St. Clare of Assisi, poverty was the only way to be united with Jesus. At the same time, her poverty was a part of the women's movement. Through her acceptance of poverty, St. Clare and her community gained autonomy and independence from the institutional church. Also, it is worth noting that the twelfth century saw the beginnings of urban life with the newly rich merchant class gaining financial power. Many peasants moved into the city and suffered from severe poverty. There was no system of infrastructure such as plumbing or heat. Most people who provided heavy labor eventually fell into poverty, sickness, and even death.

14. Amin, *Implosion of Contemporary Capitalism*, 143.

In the twenty-first century, we witness that almost everything has become privatized, and those who are uprooted from their space have little resources to support them. They fall into poverty, often with no physical space to occupy for themselves. For example, on the streets of Hong Kong tens of thousands of women domestic workers from the Philippines sit every Sunday along the sides of streets and malls, with no place to go. In Oakland, California, many people set up tents in the street and dwell in them without electricity or water. Also, we see many people living in their cars.

Traditionally, the vow of poverty is taught as a way to follow Jesus, who was on the cross in his naked body. However, we know that most religious communities do not live in complete poverty. Instead, we live in a very secure world. Most sisters have rooms and cars with professional jobs or ministry work. Even if an individual sister is poor, still the community—as an institution—has abundant resources. How, then, can we find a spirit of poverty? We presuppose that the vows themselves exist to promote our mission and sustain our call, which comes from a friendship with Jesus. From this perspective, many authors from the First World have brought several different definitions.

First, we could rename the vow of poverty as the vow of mutual sustainability.[15] The word *sustainability* considers wise and intentional uses of resources to protect the environment and humanity. The concept is deeply related to ecological concerns in the global world and possible actions vary. On a personal level, women religious try to reduce waste and compost and to share some wisdom on how to save our natural resources. On the congregational level, women religious invest in companies that are inclined towards environmental justice. The danger of this approach is losing contact with people who suffer from the environment. We are living in a world filled with images, including images of the poor and, consequently, we might lose any sense of reality. When women religious stop having direct connections

15. The idea of a vow of mutual sustainability comes from O'Murchu's *Poverty, Celibacy, and Obedience* and *Consecrated Religious Life.*

with those suffering, we cannot fully live the vow of poverty. Like water (*Tao*), women religious should go to the lower places and touch the suffering of people.

The other concept of the vow of poverty is a vow to live in simplicity. It is surprising that Jesus suggests to his disciples in the Synoptic Gospels to go simply in the context of mission, not necessarily toward monastic life. In Matthew 10 Jesus commands, "take no gold, or silver, or copper to take with you in your belts—no bag for the journey, or extra shirts, or sandals, or a staff; for the worker is worth his keep." Similarly, Mark's Gospel mentions to take nothing for the journey except a staff—no bread, no bag, no money in your belts. Wear sandals but not an extra shirt. The passage of Luke is as follows: "Take nothing for the journey—no staff, no bag, no bread, no money, no extra shirt." All three passages emphasize the necessity to not have possessions. We often understand Jesus' commands as duties or obligations, but here Jesus considers the attitude of not having things a conviction that those necessary things will be provided. Thus, the lesson of this passage regarding poverty is that it is much more a personal attitude, which focuses on relying on others and receiving their hospitality as a guest, rather than being self-sufficient.

Here, the spirit of poverty is not claiming the position of host or decision maker, but being a guest who relies on the host's hospitality. Often, we think we go into a mission or ministry field as a person in charge of the situation. Here, Jesus' teaching is the opposite. We women religious go to a mission as guests with very little control, yet with a charism, which is a gift from God and which is supposed to be given to people freely.

In Luke's Gospel, the mission discourse is repeated in chapter 10, when Jesus sends seventy-two disciples. In this discourse, Jesus repeats the same message, but adds that the disciples bring peace to the people who accept them. We can say that the gesture of being a vulnerable guest rather than host, even though the guest has the spiritual authority given by God to bring peace, is a simple expression of the vow of poverty.

As one gets older, one finds that our luggage becomes increasingly heavier. At some point, it might be inevitable that one's list of items includes medications, vast toiletries, assistance devices, and so on. But Jesus' command emphasizes what his disciples should carry: the spiritual authority to bring peace. Moreover, the simple journey suggests we women religious are not supposed to claim the position of host, but instead, we are to be guests who rely on the host.

The last expression of the vow of poverty is smallness. The German economic theorist E. F. Schumacher coined the slogan "Small is beautiful" to stand against an economic system that relied on the myth that big is successful and beautiful. Although he talked about sustainability during the energy crisis of the 1970s, the concept is even more applicable today. Simplicity as a value-driven life has become a working force for the eco-justice movement, such as having a small house, which is decidedly against the American dream, aka the Chinese dream.[16]

This theory seems to open up a new horizon of understanding of the human being and a world of limited sources. Schumacher claims that the meaning of freedom and human dignity should subsist in a sound economy based on simplicity and sustainability. If we reflect on our resentment and fear of diminishing religious communities, we can ask whether these negative feelings might come from the old paradigm which claims that big is beautiful and signifies success. In addition, it would be a blessing to women religious to be small because we could sharpen our charism and freedom within a simple lifestyle, having given up running big institutions.

In the Hebrew Scriptures, God is upset with King David asking for a census of working soldiers and punishes him and Israel severely.[17] Perhaps it is time to learn from David's experience that religious life is not a matter of quantity, but of quality. Our fundamental commitment is to follow and participate in the Jesus movement. As

16. See Schumacher, *Small Is Beautiful*.

17. See 2 Samuel 24:1–18. When he ordered the census of his soldiers, his punishment was being stricken by pestilence for three days.

one expression of poverty, if we embrace the teaching that small is beautiful, we will be equipped with the freedom and the lightness to do whatever God calls us to do with empty hands.

As such, the application of the vow of poverty is to be small and to effectively respond to the people in the world, to *delink* from the oppressive system. At the Women, Wisdom, and Action Conference, a gathering of theologian sisters from Asia and the US, the Chinese sisters created a network. They implemented a formation program in which each congregation inputs its resources to share, and poor congregations were invited for free. This action of the sisters from China is an example of sharing resources in the spirit of the joy of sharing. This kind of sharing demonstrates exactly mutual sustainability and simplicity, proclaiming the beauty of the small.

Obedience

The interpretation of obedience has changed over time, especially dramatically after the Second Vatican Council—from hierarchical to egalitarian, which means each member is to participate in decision making. Many sisters still carry wounds that they received from superiors or leadership teams in the name of obedience. Very often, we hear that a sister's dream for God and the world was shattered in the name of obedience, in setting the priority of the well-being of the community over the individual member's spiritual or physical benefit. As a consequence, many women religious refrain from serving as leaders and many communities have experienced hardships in electing leadership.

Alternatively, a high expectation for the practice of leadership repeats itself in the election of a particular circle of sisters who have administrative skills. It is common for an institutionalized or large community to have leaders who will merely manage the institutions rather than those who are visionary or change makers. The ways of electing leadership, as well as the discernment process itself, already manifest the community's predetermined direction to maintain the status quo. In this time, the vow of obedience is the most challenging of the three because it requires opening up to imagine what is yet unknown to us.

The word *obedience* is derived from the Latin word *oboedire*, which means listen. Thus, we can say that the virtue of obedience springs from the spirit of listening. If we consider religious life as living in liminal space, the language of vows will subvert its ordinary meanings in creating alternative meanings. Thus, the vow of listening will become listening to the voices of the poor and the invisible. This direction should come from the bottom to the top, not vice versa. The vow of obedience should resemble the Kenosis of Jesus, who claimed nothing as his own, although he is the All.

The vow of obedience requires not only listening to the superiors or leadership team, but also to the poor and those who are standing on the margins, in order to imagine those multicore communities. Through negating one center, the monopoly of a few can change into the cooperation of many. Some communities tend to group into small units, which gives a sense of autonomy. With this way of structuring, members of the community can listen to one another.

Also, the obedience of listening is deeply related to the vow of chastity, the vow of friendship. Through friendship with various people around the world, women religious listen to their stories of suffering and struggle and of joy and peace. Without the spirit of listening to the world and to ordinary people, our vowed life might appear very superficial or even narcissistic.

The practice of listening, ultimately, will encourage members who do not have voices to speak, as well as invite members into deeper prayer. Listening to oneself honestly is the foundation of a vowed life, and this listening can provide a profound sense of self-knowledge.

The ancient Chinese philosopher Confucius taught that the virtue of your sixties is *the taming of your ears*, so that no words irritate and, even further, that the words are heard. Some American women religious who are not used to English spoken with non-American accents demand that everyone speak a certain way.

Perhaps Confucian wisdom endeavours us to listen and to understand others, as a virtue of obedience.

The vow of obedience, which emphasizes the notion of listening, can be related to discernment. Any decision-making should be based on listening to all aspects of the situation and, more importantly, listening to the Holy Spirit, who guides us. In this process, we should include affection, reason, and thought, which will give us a sense of poise in not having to control the situation and will give us the freedom to move into a new direction. In discernment, there is no right or bad discernment, but only good and better discernment, because it is a process through which women religious—as an individual or community—can experience God's hands and deepen their orientation of life, the vowed life.

So how can we apply the vow of obedience to contemporary society, especially in light of liminality? One way to express the vow of obedience is as cultural humility. In this multicultural and interfaith world, we cannot be sure of our competency of any other culture. In addition, culture is on the move; we cannot assume that we fully understand any culture at any given moment. Women religious, like Tao or Wisdom, should become mobile and adaptable, by listening to others with sincere and humble hearts. Without limiting our understanding within the rigors of American culture, we can grow and experience transformation by engaging with and listening to others. In this spirit of obedience, we are strangers as well as hosts, and in this control-free interaction we can listen to the voice of the poor as well as the voice of God, who speaks through the cries of the oppressed and the suffering.

Chapter 5

Spirituality of the Liminal Community

Love, and do whatever you want.

—St. Augustine

Behold, how good and how pleasant it is
For brothers to dwell in unity!
It is like the fine oil upon the head
That ran down upon the beard, Upon Aaron's beard,
That ran down upon the hem of his garments;
Like the dew of Hermon
That came down upon the mountains of Zion.

—Psalm 133

The concept and understanding of community have changed greatly over the years, but they still form far from a consensus. Perhaps, what we need is not a consensus, per se, but a more accepting and varied articulation that is grounded in very specific contexts. In the world of today, many people yearn for community, or a sense of community, which can be characterized as *belonging to* as well as *engaged with*. In the midst of frequent networking, many people feel alienated and lonely. Religious life has traditionally been understood as a life of "the community." Sisters lived communally, praying, eating, and working together according to the schedule of the convent. This monastic model of religious life was so pervasive that even apostolic communities adopted this way of communal living as an essential part of religious life. Sisters wore the same dresses and veils, coming from and returning to the convent that was annexed to the schools or hospitals where they worked every day.

After the Second Vatican Council, when sisters decided to engage with the people out in the world, many religious congregations experimented with being flexible—having dinner together two or three times a week, allowing geographic freedom, and respecting sisters' ministerial environments. Further, many sisters, based on their ministerial needs, moved out to houses or apartments while at the same time keeping a strong sense of community with their sisters. Often, two sisters as a pair have maintained community life, and some sisters even have lived alone for the effectiveness of ministry. Such a diversity in the way of living shows the spirit of radical options available for mission.

This style of community living, however, is often challenging for aging members of the community. Many members who resided in small local living communities have been moved into nursing facilities, and the remaining sisters have had to readjust their living styles. Many congregations worry about how to provide retirement services to aging sisters, while still actively engaging sisters live as a single living unit. This new reality brings two different concerns. Regarding the care of older sisters, the community must have financial security, and regarding active working members, the community should provide a sense of belonging and deep spirituality of community. It is clear that the community does not necessitate always living physically together, yet it also does not exclude this possibility of living together.

We can say generally that we are now in a stage of various styles of community living, and the concept of community carries more weight than the living style of the sisters. Rather, as a characteristic of religious life, we should consider the subject of community. Thus, this chapter will explore the fundamental principles and new emerging concepts of community, and, in so doing, we will draw out the spirituality of community.

The Fundamental Concepts of Community

As women religious, we are fundamentally grounded in the Jesus movement, which was initiated at the synagogue of Nazareth, bringing the kingdom of heaven into the world. Thus, we are apocalyptic dreamers believing in the new heaven and the new earth, and community—or the principles of community—embodies this vision. It is useful to read about the early Christian church as a way to investigate the nexus of community. First, we see the fundamental dynamics of community of the early Christian community through a reading of the Acts of the Apostles. Here, community is not just a building or a governing institute, but rather a space that occurs through interaction between people who often carry different cultures, values, and identities.

Also, we elaborate charisms as a benchmark for community or community living through reading 1 Corinthians 12, Paul's renowned analogy of the body of Christ, which emphasizes diversity in unity. His teaching illuminates the principles of community in today's world of collaboration and networking.

A Reflection on the Acts of the Apostles

The text of Acts describes the process of how the early Christian community moved and grew. In the conflicted world of the first century, the burgeoning Jesus movement originated on the margins of Judea, which was subject to Roman rule and, thus, surely a source of controversy and uncertainty.[1] Imperialism exerted power through cultural and intellectual networks that operated in more invisible ways.[2] In Acts, we read how the Jesus movement challenged cultural norms as well as created an alternative world through boundary crossings.

Benchmarks of Community Living

The passage that "all who believed were together and had all things in common; they would sell their possessions and goods and distribute the proceeds to all, as any had need" (Acts 2:44–45)

1. Achtemeier et al., *Introducing the New Testament*, 266.
2. Rieger, *Christ and Empire*, 10.

historically functioned as the origin of religious community. Many rules point to this passage as the fundamental indicator for community living. For example, the Rule of St. Augustine, which is the oldest rule of religious life, emphasizes community living as the sharing of all resources.

In his Rule, St. Augustine stresses love as the priority value of community with the statement, "Love and then do whatever you want." Similarly, the Rule of St. Benedict proclaims that the monastery is a school for learning love. Although St. Augustine founded a community for priests while St. Benedict founded a monastic community, their commonality is the cultivation of community as a space for learning how to live or practice Christian love. The passage of Acts remarkably shows the fundamental value of community: cultivate love through all aspects of life.

The second point of reference for community is Acts 1:8, which shows the whole vision of the book of Acts: "You will be my witnesses in Jerusalem, in all Judea and Samaria, and to the ends of the earth." By mapping out the geographical locations, readers can recognize the expansion of the Jesus movement through multiple boundary crossings—of regions as well as cultures, religions, and ethnicities. The whole narrative begins in Jerusalem, the so-called the center of the local entity, and finishes in Rome, the center of the empire.

These two reference points of the community hold two different forces: one to cultivate and learn *within* the community; the other to go out to the world *without* the community. In this tension, Acts shows the essence of community. Within this reference of a religious community, we observe three pivotal scenes that manifest the essential aspects of the early Christian community.

The First Scene: Gaining a Voice

The first scene is the outpouring of the Holy Spirit upon the heads of the people who are praying in Jerusalem in chapter 2. It was during the feast of Pentecost, so many diaspora Jews had come to Jerusalem. The scene is about understanding foreign languages or understanding the same language spoken with heavy foreign accents by the people from the diaspora community. More specifically, the narrative of Acts explains that due to the Holy Spirit, each person there heard in their own respective tongue. Justo Gonzalez, in his commentary on Acts, insightfully explains the passage as follows:

> The Holy Spirit had two options: one was to make all understand the Aramaic the disciples spoke; the other was to make each understand in their tongue. Significantly, the Spirit chooses the latter route . . . Had the Spirit made all the listeners understand the language of the apostles, we would be justified in a centripetal understanding of mission, one in which all who come in are expected to be like those who invited them.[3]

The Holy Spirit allowed people to understand the Jesus movement or the Holy Spirit event through their vernacular languages and cultures. Often, language functions as a tool to centralize power and to regulate people's ways of thinking. In the early church, people from all over the world spoke their languages freely, and all understood them. This is the essence of the Christian community, and the grace that the Holy Spirit placed into human hearts so that they could understand or hear other languages. In so doing, many believers gained their own *authentic voices*. After receiving the Holy Spirit, people began to gather together and share their resources to construct a community, that was essentially a combination of various Hellenistic cultures.

Here, the focus is the capacity to listen to others rather than to speak for others. Confucius's *Analects* lists the virtues of listening. In chapter 2, "Governance by Virtue," he emphasizes that the virtue of being of age sixty, when a human supposedly reaches maturity, is the tamed and compliant ear. Having a tamed ear means the person can understand others without being irritated. The more we can understand the human heart, the less difficulty we feel in understanding others. When we are not bothered by others' accents or styles of talking; we can truly listen to them. In other words, when we feel at ease in listening to others, we create space

3. Gonzalez, *Acts*, 39.

for them. The most demanding people regarding speaking English might be Americans. However, in the global world many people comfortably speak English, including as their second or even third language, in their own ways. Therefore, the tamed ear is one of the most essential attitudes for being a global citizen.

The Second Scene: Crossing Borders

The second scene is located in chapters 10 and 11, wherein Peter and Cornelius, a centurion of Italian cohort, encounter each other. As a consequence of this meeting, Christians in Jerusalem accept the truth that the gospel is also accessible to Gentiles. This episode shows the principle of building intercultural communities, which was the nature of the early Christian church. Remarkably, in this episode, there is no "other," which often referred to the position of the margin or the minor. In the midst of the power of the Holy Spirit, the whole narrative is balanced so that there is not a single subject that can be considered as a counterpart to the other. Instead, the scene shows an intersubjectivity between Peter and Cornelius in mutual respect. The flow of the Spirit from the Godhead challenges the sociocultural norms and invites Peter and new Jesus followers into a place of unfamiliarity.

In the first part of this episode, Peter sees a vision impelling him to cross the boundary of dietary codes, and the undoing of food restrictions becomes organically related to the acceptance of Gentiles. Peter, who had received a stranger/guest at the lodge where he stayed as a guest, visits Cornelius, the stranger under the law of the Holy Spirit. In this encounter, there is a thin line between the host and the guest, or more accurately described, neither is the host nor the guest. They are equally open to the power of the Holy Spirit. This event signifies the crossing of boundaries of ethnicities, religions, and cultures.

In the first-century Greco-Roman world, Cornelius and Peter lived with class differences. Cornelius's sociopolitical position was much higher than that of Peter, an ordinary Jew who was subjected to Roman rule. However, in their interaction, there was only respect, with Peter solely focused on God's voice with no thought of his inferior social position. Likely, Cornelius took no entitlements from empire officials. Rather, his sole concern was God's invitation. With it, he is willing to cross any borders, including class, for this alternative way of living.

However, the greatest surprise from this episode is that Cornelius and his colleagues receive the Holy Spirit in a mysterious way, which reveals the freedom of God. So Peter suggests that they be baptized, reversing the process of becoming a member of the Christian community, in which receiving the Holy Spirit follows baptism. In this way, the text emphasizes the freedom of the Spirit that flows from the Godhead. In this border crossing, Peter and Cornelius both must admit the leadership of the Spirit, thereby giving up their own culture and procedures. The second scene reveals the Jesus movement, which reverses or subverts orders, rules, and structures, and which includes various aspects of border crossings. As a principle for intercultural community building, border crossing is essential.

The Final Scene: Self-Emptying

The final scene is in chapter 15, namely the Jerusalem council. The burgeoning community created a discerning space in which they ponder what happened to the Jesus movement, following the flow of the Holy Spirit. The Jewish Christians who belong to the Pharisees raised issues regarding the requirement of circumcision and the Mosaic law (15:5). It is clear that there were Jewish Christians who observed Moses' law, as well as other Jewish rules, and Acts describes dissonances in the community in a neutral tone, implying that the quarrels and disagreements are not obstacles to the Jesus movement. Instead, the real obstacle was the attitude of not listening to the Holy Spirit or to one another. In this episode, Jerusalem becomes the borderland or the in-between space where all discomfort, ambiguity, and uncertainty remain, and where the community can make decisions through the Spirit-filled process of discernment.

The word discernment is derived from the Latin *discernere*, meaning "separate." In this episode, the church community must separate cultural practices from gospel values. Additionally, they have to measure crucial or essential rules, not from their own cultural comfort but rather from the Gentile perspective. Here Peter employs the basic logic that as grace was given to them by the Holy Spirit, so it was to Gentiles. In verse 11 he emphasizes the importance of God's freedom, which we can neither be predicted nor stopped, referring to his own lived experience.

The council thus concludes that each local community will keep minimal requirements, proclaiming that the Gentile Christian church does not have to mimic Jewish ways and in so doing the Christian church can openly admit diversity. The four minimal prohibitions will function to unify Jewish Christians with Gentile Christians.[4] The fruits of discernment may have implied that the local church would gain more autonomy when guided by the Holy Spirit, and this decision would usher the Christian movement onto the next stage to flourish on Mediterranean soil. After this event, the center becomes the margin, and the margin becomes the center. Any place, then, can be the center and/or the margin interchangeably.

Applying the spirit of Acts to community life, we can conclude that our community living or dwelling in liminal space includes fundamentally crossing boundaries in order to embrace diversity, to listen to others in the spirit of Jesus, and to flexibly be both the center and the margin through self-emptying.

Charism

The other fundamental criterion of community is the charism that each community epitomizes. As we mentioned earlier, if the community is the indicator of cultivating love through crossing boundaries and self-emptying, then charism is the unique and creative expression of the community.

4. Savelle, "Reexamination of the Prohibitions in Acts 15," 465–66.

Today, many congregations and communities are involved in intercongregational ministries. For example, the Social Justice and Peace Network is composed of twelve congregations and works for social justice and peace on a global scale. Some people might ask why each community still needs a charism if we are becoming more collaborative and smaller in size. Some sisters predict that we will all become one congregation someday. Actually, in France, sisters have been trying to create one community because of their rapidly diminishing numbers.

However, our charism is a driving force for creating a spirit of community in terms of diversity and difference. In the New Testament, Paul describes the beauty of variety in unity, in the First Letter to the Corinthians, chapter 12. He says, "For just as the body is one and has many parts, and all its many parts form one body, so it is with Christ" (v. 12) . . . as it is, God arranged the parts in the body, each of them, as he chose" (v. 18). We believe that this passage claims the beauty of diversity as the fundamental discipline of community. As a whole, religious communities need different charisms, each with unique functions in creating love.

When we work together, we need diversity. Paul further explains the importance of diversity by saying, "If all were one part, where would the body be? As it is, there are many parts, but one body." (vv. 19–20). If we all chose one part, it would become a monopoly or something resembling imperialism. If we follow only effectiveness and productivity, even for the sake of goodness, we would suffocate the spirit of diversity and the minority expression would succumb to the big congregations.

In this regard, we should probably ask what determines bigness—is it the number of members, the number of younger members, or the amount of financial resources? One countercultural and prophetic work that women religious perform for the world is rejecting any representation of religious life, not losing unique differences. Liminal space can be the place for new voices and new songs. In this sense, charisms will create a new song, which will make diverse variations of its own.

In the scriptures, we find that leaders who are chosen by God are often perplexed, asking, "Did God really call me, someone who belongs to a small or humble tribe?" Again, we are invited to worry about numbers, resources, and productivity. Charisms are gifts to the world that encourage diversity without the loss of individual or minority voices.

It is very common for a religious community to work with lay partners, as well as associates or third-order members. Its charism is the initial invitation to walk together for mission as well as for the formation of new members. It helps explain how each new member, and any type of partner in ministry, is invited into a certain aspect of mission as given by the Holy Spirit. Each charism with its unique flavor should be explored within a concrete context. For example, the charism of CCVI—to make the merciful love of the incarnated Word a real and tangible presence in the world to-day—should be elaborated on as a way to communicate with those people with whom the community engages. As such, the charism of SNJM—the full development of the human person—should be reiterated constantly according to the time and location.

Charism is not a set of sealed documents, but rather the living flesh of each religious community. Along with a new language for the understanding of vows, we also need a new language of charism. Surplus meaning can be created in the process of sharing stories. Understanding and appropriating the story of charism, which is always retold in various contexts, enriches the meaning of charism, and a charism based on many shared stories will provide a life-giving well from which to draw.

Emerging Concepts of Community

In the twenty-first century, we find many people, both young and old, yearning for a community in which they can collaborate and create new ways of being. However, the pace and ways of constructing community is quite different from the past. As such, we would like to use the borderland, a porous place where various interactions happen constantly, but with the community working as its foundation.

First, community living in the borderland means a shared governance, which means that all constituencies of the institution participate in and are informed in decision making and policies. In general, the stake holders are meant to share in information. For shared governance, the most demanding virtues are transparency, fairness, and communication. For women religious communities, collaboration with other congregations, lay people, and anyone who shares their vision for the world has become the new normal.

On this path, all information and knowledge should be shared in a timely and effective manner with all constituencies involved. For that, communication is a prerequisite, as sharing knowledge will function as the anchor for creating community and developing actions.[5]

The other concern for community or communal actions in the borderland is networking through a multifocal structure. Community building often means having religious communities joining the center or having access to the center. This way of community building could be linear and hierarchical, which has merits for conveying ideas very quickly, but also has the fatal weakness of not including many voices or opinions. This multifocal community structure means that members share power with one another, and that shared ideas can move to other circles or communities more easily. If we exist to spread gospel values as an alternative way of living, it seems obvious to move to this multifocal structure.

The birthday paradox shows the benefits of a multiple-centered structure of community. In probability theory, the birthday paradox looks at the probability that in a set of twenty-three randomly chosen people, some will share the same birthday. On the surface, the possibility looks very low. However, the comparisons of birthdays is actually made between every possible pair of individuals—23 x 22 / 2 = 253, which is more than half the number of days in a year—as opposed to being fixed on one individual and

5. Shirky, *Here Come Everybody*, 47.

comparing their birthday to everyone else's birthday.[6] This theory gives a different outlook for understanding the power of possibility when people interact.

How can we imagine community life in light of the birthday paradox? Women religious are decreasing in numbers, yet we can still be mutually interactive in sharing information and decision making. We believe the future of religious life can expect this kind of interactive and pluralistic interactions to enhance social justice. These days, many family members and friends want to support the poor in the Third World. If women religious had a network to link people around the globe, it could be the function of the community of women religious.

Finally, the new way of community living will be mobility, indicating both a mental and physical ability to move. Mental mobility means the flexibility to adapt a new way of being in community. Technology changes our mental acuity, and the younger generation does not use handwriting or show much enthusiasm for reading written material. In my class, students do not pay much attention to printed material, preferring to read through a screen. Class teachings are delving into increasingly online-based learning. More people would rather text than use email or snail mail. It is not a matter of good or bad, but a matter of fact. Facebook is used less by younger generations (e.g., millennials), who prefer Snapchat or Instagram; they are image driven rather than text driven. Tech companies are quick and skillful at navigating how to communicate with the world. For example, Google recently stopped operating Google+ because of a lack of users.

Community life means using social media, through which we have access to communicate. In today's world, many women religious communities provide workshops for sisters so that they can stay updated on technology, and many committee meetings and gatherings are done virtually. Especially for international congregations, mobility through technology has become more crucial.

Given these realities, what is physical mobility? Women religious in the US tend to think that the obvious location for

6. "Birthday Paradox," paras. 9–11.

meetings is the US. Of course, this country has great resources to support any kind of gathering, but it does not mean that we should not go to other places. Also, whenever we meet, the official language is English, assuming that everyone speaks English, and the American methods of running meetings are often applied to non-American counterparts.

Cross-cultural communication, including meeting facilitation, as an art of the borderland should subvert the center and explore the margins. Women religious must go to other places, beyond US borders, and participate in meetings run in other languages. Then those experiences will open the sisters up to a new level of understanding the other, as well as of their own self-centeredness.

The Spirituality of Community as Liminal Living

The spirituality of community, which is located in liminal space, is border-crossing spirituality and borderland spirituality in the context of religious life. Spirituality is an ongoing action of the interpretation of our lived experience.[7] Regarding religious life as a way of living in community or of communal living, we would elaborate the spirituality of community and include elements of both the old and new ways of community. Because an articulation of spirituality is the process of reflecting on the present, when we explore spirituality, we should keep in mind that spirituality lives in the *here and now.*

Our current global neoliberal context reflects a monopolizing capital system and a growing disparity between the poor and the rich, as well as a very rapidly changing way of being due to technology. Also, it reflects our own smallness, in losing many great members with deep capability to handle difficult situations and spiritual wisdom. Like Israel wandering in the desert and preparing to enter Canaan, we are losing good leaders, wisdom teachers, and perhaps glorious institutions that we have

7. Schneiders, "Christian Spirituality," 47.

inherited. Our sorrow, embarrassment, and frustration should be fully embraced in this spirituality of community, without shame, and without a rushed hope.

This spirituality of community means a group of women religious who carry a distinct charism. However, the community is not a closed system but is rather open and porous so that various types of memberships can operate in the system. Each community is open to collaboration with other communities and open to inviting various partners, including lay people or any global citizens who wish to work together on a particular project.

Community might then look like any random social justice activist group or a lay person volunteering with a mission. However, religious people are women who stand within a continuous commitment that comes from each one's call by God, to work for the kingdom of heaven. In a conclusive manner, we elaborate the spirituality of community in the twenty-first century.

Kenosis

We see the Greek word *kenosis*, which indicates Jesus' self-emptying action, in Philippians 2:7. Every Good Friday, we sing the hymn of Jesus, who died for our salvation on the cross. After the liturgy, the church enters a liminal space that continues until the Easter Vigil. Thus, liturgically speaking, this hymn manifests the spirituality of the religious community, which is on the journey from the desert to the promised land, analogous to the contemporary world.[8] Actually, this hymn was supposedly already spreading among the burgeoning Christian communities when Paul inserted it in his letter. We believe that this song was popular because it captures the core of the spirituality of the emerging communities.

When I teach the class on "Social Justice and Spirituality," I ask students to bring one hip-hop or pop song that conjures up for them a sense of social justice or spirituality or both. We then enjoy listening to the chosen music and analyzing the lyrics

8. The theme of journey from desert to the future comes from Catherine M. Harmer. See Harmer, *Religious Life in the 21ˢᵗ Century*.

together and, in so doing, try to make sense of the meaning of social justice. Popular songs, as social criticism, bring their message to the world. Students bring songs like the Black Eyed Peas' "Where Is the Love?" and Bob Marley's "Get Up Stand Up" very often. One student brought the K-pop band BTS's "Love Yourself." College students find that songs resonate with their fears, disappointments, and hopes.

Thus, we can see that the hymn or the song in the letter to the Philippians resonates with the spirit of the community. As we know, the letter is very joyful, and Paul appreciates the friendship through which he and the community work together, helping the Jerusalem church and providing hospitality. In the spirit of friendship of deep trust, Paul imagines singing this song together.

Also, this song has had a canonical position in Christian communities for a long time. Its message has been constantly interpreted as the core tenet of the Christian community. As such, in the spirit of friendship, the song brings a deep spirituality, yet still remains open to possibilities of surplus meaning that emerge through an engagement with the song.

The song can be read as emphasizing a self-emptying action, as a way to fill up with other people. This spirituality is fundamentally christocentric, but is more inclusive of the human aspect of Jesus. Actually, the term *kenosis* indicates the divine love embodied in the body of the Galilean Jesus. In the Letter to the Philippians, Paul exclaims, "In Christ Jesus, who, though he was in the form of God, did not count equality with God a thing to be grasped, but emptied himself, taking the form of a servant, being born in the likeness of men. And being found in human form he humbled himself and became obedient unto death, even death on a cross" (2:6–8).

This song was inserted, so it is plausible that the hymn was taught by Paul to the people in Philippi. The whole structure of the hymn is bipartite, with the theme of lowliness (2:6–8) and exaltation (2:9–11). Raymond Brown explains that in 2:6–7 Jesus, "who being in the form of God," did not think himself equal to God as a *harpagmon* (something to be clung to or grasped at), and emptied himself, having become or been born in a human form.[9] Here, the most interesting word is *harpagmon*. The negative action that Jesus takes in this hymn is not to cling to his identity. Rather, Jesus' non-attachment to his own or true identity is the very definition of *kenosis*; we never arrive at the level of *kenosis*.

However, we can think of at least letting go or detaching from values or possessions that give us identity as women religious in the US. We are used to being respected in the church and having well-known ministries. Sometimes our sense of security comes from a sense of familiarity, and that familiarity tends to be exclusive and clinging to like-minded people, such as those of the same age, background, or race. Fully admitting that we cannot practice *kenosis* as the mystery that Jesus was incarnated, we can also admit our attachment to familiar environments or old mental positions. In the time of leadership in transition and new religious life, our spirituality should be detachment from a familiar past and an opening up to new unknown possibilities. Just as young university students adapt to their new campus environment, we too need to practice this attitude.[10] In other words, the spirituality of *kenosis* is an active determination to walk into the mystery of the unknown and uncertain, in trust of God, until we dare to lose our identity.

Behold

One of the most fascinating words in the Bible is *behold*, which itself is an empty word, but one that gently nudges the reader into a deeper meaning. The function of the word hints at the meaning of liminal space, which includes possibilities for transformative meaning. For elaborating on the meaning of *behold*, the chosen passage comes from the first chapter of Luke's Gospel. The implied readers of Luke's Gospel were the people of the global church in the first century, which was actively flowing, mobile, and adaptable. I find the social location of these readers to be similar to our

---

9. Brown, *Introduction to the New Testament*, 492.

10. Sivalon, "Gift of Uncertainty," 12–13.

own social location. Interestingly, this global salvation epic begins with a local narrative of a young lady who lives in a small town called Nazareth in Galilee. Here, Mary stands in the midst of the mystery, but yet not fully understanding it. The process of understanding the mystery in the global world begins with Mary's own process of understanding her vocation.

The Location of the Pericope

The all-too-familiar scenes in 1:5–25 and 1:26–38, commonly known under the titles "Annunciation to Zechariah" and "Annunciation to Mary," adhere to Luke's use of the literary form of the birth announcement. These two stories recount the news of the miraculous births of two children as proclaimed by the same heavenly messenger, Gabriel.[11] In this parallel structure, we can see as follows:

A (Annunciation to Zechariah)—1: 5–25

A' (Annunciation to Mary)—1: 26—2:3

B (Mary Visits Elizabeth)—1: 39–56

C (Birth of John)—1: 57–80

C' (Birth of Jesus)—2:1–20

Fig. 1. The Parallel Structure of the Pericope

We can say that story A exists to highlight A', without eliminating the importance of A. More importantly, this moment of A' empowers Mary to take an action and engage with other, which is the main theme of the whole introduction.

For many feminist biblical scholars, Luke's narrative, in general, is suspicious because the narrative pays attention to women but gives women only a minor role, as the beneficiaries of Jesus' ministry rather than as his companions. But this is a rare passage, in that it deals with women characters seriously, although many scholars argue Mary is not a central figure here because

11. Feník and Lapko, "Annunciation to Mary," 498.

her role is limited to bearing a child.[12] However, I do not believe the Mary in this passage is passive. Her role is crucial because her fertile body becomes a vehicle for delivering the Savior. In this pericope, Mary asks, challenges, ponders, and accepts her vocation—which is uncertain and overwhelming—and initiates her action. The whole mood in Luke's annunciation is not heavy with moral dilemma but rather with celebration and joy. Through this process, Mary glimpses the mystery, and the celebration is complete when she encounters and collaborates with Elizabeth and sings the song of the Magnificat. Actually, many ancient texts put the song on Elizabeth's lips.[13] But it does not matter who owns the song; the two women create it together as companions in the salvific drama, creating a unison.

The Glimpse of the Mystery

How Mary grasped the mystery is deeply related to her own understanding of self and others. The chosen periscope explains how Mary reaches a level of understanding. A person who understands the mystery is one who sees reality, truth, and perhaps God's plan. In this passage, the process of seeing the mystery is intertwined with the word *behold*. Throughout chapters 1 and 2 of Luke's Gospel, we find the word *behold* used ten times. In the United Bible Society's Greek New Testament,[14] the word appears as καί ιδου ("and behold"). Some manuscripts omit ιδου and this word is considered an ellipse, which includes the whole context yet omits an explanation, and both does and does not guide readers into the next event or character. Thus, we can say the word *behold* signifies meaning, yet omits it at the same time. In this way, it creates an in-between space of understanding the mystery.

The Latin word used for the word *behold* is *ecce*. In John 19:6, the text says *ecce homo,* and the word *ecce* directly points at Jesus

---

12. Schaberg, "Luke," in *Women's Bible Commentary*, 372.

13. Metzger, *Textual Commentary*, 111.

14. Metzger, *Textual Commentary*, 18.

or indicates seeing Jesus, with no further explanation. Also, the word *ecce* signifies "here," emphasizing the present moment, yet is an elliptical meaning in an exclamative mode. This word *behold*, then, can be understood as "the empty signifier," the term created by psychoanalyst Jacques Lacan, which evokes a chain of symbols and meanings, including a great level of resistance and suspicion, as much as emptying or omitting while also suggesting walking into a deeper level of mystery.[15]

The word *behold* comes from the Old English word *bihaldan*, which is composed of *bi* and *haldan* and carries the meaning "hold thoroughly" or "thoroughly remain." Thus, the meaning of *behold* is identical to a well-known definition of contemplation, "a long and loving gaze at the real," according to Water Burghardt. Yet, the word *behold* is not a full signifier. Rather, it is an empty word with a full gesture of mutual invitation, not forcing others but seeking intimate interaction. I believe this behold invites us into and indicates the mystery of God's salvation, which unfolds through Mary's—or the reader's—self-knowledge and conscientious action.

In self-emptying actions or in interactions with others, we can voluntarily lose entitlement or our American-centeredness in front of people from around the globe. In the gaze of beholding, women religious can be a part of the world, engaging with people and participating in matters of justice and peace.

Freedom: Letting Go, Letting Come

Finally, the spirituality of community can be found in the spirit of freedom, which exists in the in-between space of "letting go" and "letting come." In this whirling present reality, we must learn the spirit of letting go and, at the same time, of letting come. Several years ago, the animated film *Frozen* was very popular, especially the song, "Let It Go." The lyrics for the refrain are as follows:

---

15. See Lacan, *Seminar XI*, 67.

Let it go, let it go
Can't hold it back anymore
Let it go, let it go
Turn away and slam the door . . . .

It's funny how some distance makes everything seem small
And the fears that once controlled me can't get to me at all
It's time to see what I can do
To test the limits and break through
No right, no wrong, no rules for me
I'm free.[16]

Here, Elsa decides to let go of everything. As a process for becoming whole, the young woman slams the door in order to become herself. However, the true spirit of letting go does not end with shutting down her mind and freeing herself from judgment or fear. Maybe a sense of freedom will subsequently create a space for letting come—of anything we do not anticipate, maybe sad suffering or maybe joyful surprise. In the spirituality of community, which originates from a space for cultivating love, we need courage for letting go, and for letting come.

The Sufi writer Rumi's poem "The Guest House" provides us with a perspective regarding the freedom to let go and let come:

This being human is a guest house.
Every morning a new arrival.

A joy, a depression, a meanness,
some momentary awareness comes
as an unexpected visitor.

Welcome and entertain them all!
Even if they are a crowd of sorrows,
Who violently sweep your house

Empty of its furniture,
still, treat each guest honorably.
He may be clearing you out
For some new delight.

16. Menzel, "Let It Go," paras. 1–2.

The dark thought, the shame, the malice,
Meet them at the door laughing and inviting them in.

Be grateful for whoever comes,
Because each has been sent
As a guide from beyond.[17]

Community is a school for love, and the spirituality of letting go and letting come is the foundation and summit of the spirituality of *kenosis*, beholding, and freedom to let go and let come—these three aspects of spirituality intersect with one another. In twenty-first-century religious life, community still holds a central place, no matter how we practice community living.

The community is an expression of and a commitment to love, which comes from a relationship with God and engagement with the Jesus movement. The spirituality of the liminal community lies in the action of all members, and it can be actualized in the spirit of self-emptying, beholding, and letting go and letting come, in which women religious would be free agents to actively participate in the Jesus movement.

17. Rumi, "Guest House," lines 1–17.

Border-Crossing Leadership

Leaders are the ones who run headfirst into the unknown.
They rush toward the danger.
They put their own interests aside to protect us
or to pull us into the future.

—"Leaders Eat Last" by Simon Sinek

Leadership is like a handful of water.
Lord, let us be the people to share it with those who thirst.

—"A Leader's Prayer" by unknown author

In terms of leadership, women religious have been superb. Most of the community leaders have been trained well in planning, structuring, and maintaining. There is no doubt that the leadership style of the religious community is far more democratic than other communities of other countries. In the US, many congregations are undergoing reconfiguration or merging due to the current situation of decreasing membership and aging. In this process, many sisters are experiencing dislocation and dissonance. Often, most victims are members of the first formation process, wherein no clear guidelines and differing messages were given by various community members.

Most leaders in the religious communities of women were champions in accepting feminist ideas, and in emphasizing egalitarian and discerning spirits. Nevertheless, many leaders have to handle a large volume of managerial and administration materials, and are busy with participation in staff and board meetings, as well as taking care of elderly members. Aging sisters who are independent and self-determined do not want to move houses or give up driving. Sisters in leadership positions must handle these situations with aged members with tender and kind hearts.

A New Way of Leadership

It is undeniable that congregations have hope for the future, but the current leadership teams do not seem to reflect much on this concern. The process of decision making in the contemplative mode often means moving at a snail's pace, so that full-time working members cannot be part of the implementation. At this slow pace, it is generally the retired sisters who are the center of the process, which then reflects their experiences rather than the experiences of members currently in the field. The work looks very contemplative and intuitive, yet we should remember that when we name something as intuitive, or intuitively right, we often mean it is just familiar. In other words, in all their operative systems, the discerning process reflects the system that women religious developed and that mostly fits in with the experience of the majority of sisters who are now in their eighties. Observing my religious community, as well as many other communities, the election of leadership seems to be predetermined with a specific type of leadership—mainly management and maintenance.

In the dawn of a new way of religious life in the twenty-first century, we must address some critical questions: Do we trust that God's wisdom is in motion, passing into the souls of the next generation and calling them to leadership? Do we notice that God's wisdom is beginning to renew everything in the leadership of those few brave younger members in our midst? Can we boldly reject all aspects of the thinking process and open to a new one?[1]

In the last decades, LCWR has spent much time considering the role of leaders in religious congregations. In the US, leadership has been a good model for lay men and women who are committed to the church and the world. In a word, this leadership can

1. Maya, "Called to Leadership," 160–61.

be "transformational leadership," with a set of dispositions, a way of being in the world, that creates an environment for a profound and authentic transformation of the individual and of the whole.[2] The leadership of the future, many authors note, must emphasize contemplative leadership with a discerning spirit as well as a prophetic imagination.

Based on these insights, we will elaborate on the essential aspect of leadership in the context of the twenty-first century. The current time can be called "the age of the multitude." The term *multitude*, as coined by Michael Hardt and Antonio Negri, explains active social subjects who participate in the creation of an alternative world, as a resistance to a global capitalism based on singularities.[3] This concept is useful to understand the contemporary human subject who decides all activities individually, which can operate collaboratively through networking. In today's society, globalization is not a matter of everyone in the world becoming the same. Instead, it provides the possibility that, while remaining different, we willl discover the commonality that enables us to communicate and act together.[4]

The concept of the multitude can be identified by a new approach to religious life as a network among sisters. Hardt and Negri explain further that the "multitude too might thus be conceived as a network: an open and expansive network in which all differences can be expressed freely and equally, a network that provides the means of the encounter so that we can work and live in common."[5] In the twenty-first century, human society consists of the multitudes, and as congruence, the religious community would consist of the multitudes who retain unique characteristics, yet create universal unity. This ideal is, as a matter of fact, identical to the ideal of Paul, diversity in unity (1 Cor 12).

New leaders would be very different from what our religious communities are accustomed to. We would feel at home with a

2. Sanders, ed., *Transformational Leadership*, xi.

3. Hardt and Negri, *Multitude*, 100.

4. Hardt and Negri, *Multitude*, 2.

5. Hardt and Negri, *Multitude*, 2.

smaller religious life, never having been part of the large cohorts, and we were formed in collaboration from our early years, having friendships among the few in our age groups across our congregational spectrums. Our DNA has a different composition; our leadership style will also be different.[6] New wine needs a new wineskin, and this direction requires much new research from theology as well as another field of work, such as community organization, management, social psychology, and education.

The Leadership Models for Small Congregations

At a gathering of Asian women religious dedicated to doing theology, I conversed with a sister from an international congregation small enough to be interconnected in various ministries, reflecting global concerns. She told me that her community had always had fewer than two hundred members, and thus it had never been a challenge to discern together and work together. There is no such thing as a perfect community, but at least all members of her community directly engaged in the decision-making process and participated in the ministries.

Because of environmental concerns, poverty, and the disproportionate accumulation of wealth with a lack of morality for shared wealth and a just distribution of resources, now E. F. Schumacher's *Small Is Beautiful* brings our attention to smallness.[7] As a scholar of the economy of the seventies, he argues for the importance of sustainability, criticizing the culture of appreciating bigness as a scale of success. Schumacher challenges the notion of success, which has become more prominent, by elaborating a new value of mutual sustainability.

In many areas of the earth, some from the younger generation now accept and adopt this principle, and try to live intentionally in a small way. They commute to work by bike and purchase smaller houses, thereby guaranteeing a lower cost of living. Also,

6. Maya, *In Our Own Words*, 160.
7. Schumacher, *Small Is Beautiful*.

there has emerged a natural community among younger people living in smaller individual spaces with shared common spaces, to create a sense of community. Instead of limiting their households to children, parents, and grandparents, plenty of people are going a step further, making homes with friends and even strangers.

The journalist Ilana E. Strauss explains the current trend of cohousing, in which a large community lives together and shares household duties. In these settings, individuals or families generally have their own houses, bedrooms, or apartments but share things like kitchens and community spaces.[8] They commonly trade off responsibilities like cooking and gardening. This lifestyle shows a creatively constructed living condition that emphasizes being small and being sustainable. An emerging new way of religious life would be coherent with this cohousing movement, in terms of sustainability and being small.

Transitional Leadership Models

We would say that we are in the midst of a transition from a big institution to a small community, although the median age of the majority of members are in the eighties. For the congregation of the Sisters of Holy Names of Jesus and Mary, which is certainly transitioning from a big institution to a small community, some of the congregational and provincial leaders have decided to only serve part-time. In regarding the current numbers of active members, the community acknowledged, for the first time, that its leadership did not require full-time commitment. Instead, some sisters continue their mission while serving as leaders of the community. It reflects the wisdom of caring for the institution property as well as older members, while the leadership team sisters also keep their sense of mission and ministry, and all while inviting younger sisters to leadership roles.

The other type of transitional leadership model invites younger sisters to practice conventions. In this model, the newly

---

8. Strauss, "Hot New Millennial Housing Trend," para. 4.

chosen younger generation of leaders learn a breadth of manage-rial skills, including funeral planning. We believe the leaders in this stage should take the role of a bridge between the old gen-eration and the new emerging generation. In this case, the most challenging aspect is supporting those few leaders chosen to serve the community, who can easily feel lonely and tired because they often handle the generational gap.

An alternative model is a two-tier or dual-leadership model. One tier represents a group of sisters composed of retired mem-bers, with the leader of this tier being responsible for managing resources. The leadership team of the tier takes care of aged mem-bers, and the housing and well-being of the sisters. The lived legacy of the older members will be remembered through well-managed funerals and a caring dying process. Sisters who take care of old members should communicate frequently and efficiently with the other sisters who belong to the other tier. The leadership team also supervises investing resources to promote sustainability.

The other tier focuses on the current mission and its future. The leadership team of this tier plans and performs the formation of members, and implements a new mission plan with sisters in other areas of the world—enhancing mission and cultivating spiri-tuality in the twenty-first century through global networking and collaboration. For this, encouragement to new ministries is strongly required, as well as a bold spirit of letting go. Even missions that have given the congregation fame and success in the past, if it is no longer life-giving or does not function as it should, should be given up. Once we let go, then we can discern what is opening up.

The two-tier model is manifested in the Acts of the Apostles, in which the disciples experience the transition from a local com-munity to a global church. Early Christianity had a two-tier lead-ership: one tier was in Jerusalem under the leadership of Peter and James; the other tier was in Antioch under the leadership of Paul and Barnabas. While the Jerusalem church kept a Jewish Christian identity, in which they tried to integrate Jesus' teachings within the Jewish tradition, the Antioch church followed the Holy Spirit, who guided them into an unknown world, creating a global mission church. In Acts, Barnabas and Paul go to Jerusalem several times, for mutual discernment for inviting the Gentiles to the church, as well as for reports on the mission communities. Also, later burgeoning communities, such as Antioch and Philippi, provided financial support to the Jerusalem church. It is clear that two-tier leaders were united in the Holy Spirit, although they performed with different leadership roles.

It is crucial at this transitional moment of congregations that there is an inner freedom to discern a direction and model of leadership to fit each congregation. For now, leaders need to set predefined objectives and find clear road maps. Also, most importantly, leaders should facilitate well-planned and prayerful dialogues among members, acknowledging that the religious community is getting smaller and, therefore, more beautiful, in that we can run for mission in a global world.

Shared Leadership Model

In the future, leadership will be a more shared model, in which each member is a leader. This form comes from Numbers 11:24–30, which is a hint of ideal leadership in Israel. In the wildness, Moses brings together seventy elders and has them stand around the tent. Then God takes some of the power of the Spirit that was on Moses and puts it on the seventy. As a consequence, the Spirit rests on them and they prophesy. This episode shows that centralized leadership was resisted in Hebrew Scriptures, along with Judges and 1 and 2 Samuel. The more obvious message is stated through Moses: "I wish that all the Lord's people were prophets and that the Lord would put his Spirit on them!" (Num 11:29, NIV).

The currently operating model of shared leadership in religious institutions and congregations is in the form of a delegation to the committees. Committee work is a way to give space to a group of members to focus on particular work. The weakness of this committee model is its rigid boundary. If a sister does not belong to a particular committee, she does not know much about the decision-making process. For example, if we have a committee dedicated to formation, the committee focuses on the formation of younger members. The strength of this model lies in professionalism, as most of the community will undoubtedly choose those who are experts in education and have skills. This could be good, in theory, but most members will likely feel excluded and could easily remain passive.

Given this, what kind of leadership model might fit into the emerging religious life? The younger generation is not used to being passive recipients. In most college classrooms, faculty find that millennial students want to participate in the learning process, as they are not used to listening to lectures, even if they are well prepared. At Holy Names University in California, one of the most diverse colleges in the US, students asked the school to not only teach ethnic studies courses, but to also change humanities courses so that they can gain knowledge from perspectives other than European. Also, the new generation knows how to work together effectively and creatively, not necessarily based on division.

I believe the religious community leadership model can reflect the reality of the young generation, so that we can create a multifocal model rather than a committee model. This would emphasize many leaders in the community and create a polity.[9] The multifocal model, as a shared leadership style, invites every member to participate in multiple agendas. As long as the concern or agenda is attractive, any member can be a part of the group. Also, the process of decision making will manifest at a virtual bulletin, where the collection of ideas happens, as any member can put their topics on there.

Wikipedia, an open platform to create knowledge, is a showcase of a new way of operating. Years ago, many teachers rejected any references from Wikipedia. However, its quality is constantly improving because it operates as an open system in which anyone can add content, make edits, and correct the knowledge created. Wikipedia is an example of a multifocal model, emphasizing everyone as participants and creating knowledge as a process. In the

9. Weibel, "People, Politics, and Power," 31.

operating model of Wikipedia, anyone can add an idea, and if it does not gain support the thread will quickly disappear.

Religious communities can adapt the Wikipedia operation mode into their leadership models. As such, leaders are not limited; rather, women religious could participate in all areas and share volumes of ideas. Any member can choose to be the leader according to the theme, and it will be flexible. Here sisters will work together with other groups freely as well as collaborating with sisters of the same community.

Research on the effects of shared leadership shows that the shared leadership style, as a process-oriented leadership, has a positive impact on team effectiveness by promoting teamwork and shared mentality among members. Shared leadership enhances effective group decision making among team members, through their sharing of diverse knowledge. The leaders who tend to share leadership styles also facilitate the development of a close relationship among members. Thus, leaders using a shared leadership style can share their vision and, in this way, sharing leadership increases members' passion for the project.[10]

In addition to shared responsibilities, as a small congregation, all members share information and the decision-making process through communication skills. In this way, the leadership role is not any more representative, but all members share equal responsibility for creating the future. The unique element of the suggested shared leadership exists in the porous boundary between projects. In a sense, leadership stands as interstitial space, not claiming a person as the leader. Rather, everyone is an equal stakeholder and all carry the task together. In these small communities, the leadership or participation intersects often. The idea will become clearer through the intersection and, at the same time, the idea expands.

10. Choi et al., "Effects of Transformative and Shared Leadership Styles," 385.

The Assets of Being a Border-Crossing Leader

What kind of a profile is necessary for border-crossing leadership? Many organization studies in business school list several assets to be an effective leader. Although those studies are secular, they surprisingly discuss the spirituality of leadership. Their general requirements are: creating a vision, serving the stakeholders, and building an organization to deliver those things. However, rather than being a position with a long list of functional responsibilities, leadership can more accurately be described as a mindset, a way of being that reflects how one views the world, who one is, and what one wants to do in and for it.[11] In this perspective, the spirituality of leadership is about multiplying resources, managing uncertainty, and networking. We do not mean this asset as a skill, but a spirituality as a summary of actions, orientations, and thought processes.

Multiplying Resources

We all have experiences of a leader who has discouraged us, rejecting our ideas or plans. Also, we have had dead-end moments in which we had a passion for a new project and presented it to the leader, and the leader listened, with no action taken whatsoever. They even showed no emotion, so that we did not know whether or not the leader supported us. Then, with the leader's lack of reaction, our passion died out. This kind of leader is a diminishing leader.

Researcher in the field of leadership Liz Wiseman interviewed more than one hundred management team members and coined the term *multipliers* about those leaders who make others geniuses, rather than being the geniuses themselves.[12] The multipliers fundamentally believe that people are so smart they will figure something out and get even smarter in the process. Thus, the role of the leader is to create a safe space that liberates people's best thinking and then to get out of their way.[13] On the contrary, di-

---

11. Benezet, *Journey of Not Knowing*, 44.

12. Wiseman, *Multipliers*, 5.

13. Wiseman, *Multipliers*, 20.

minishing leaders are those who set the limits of ideas and assume that no one will have solutions. Here, those leaders have a fixed mindset; their way of doing something should be a certain way, in which the leader feels comfortable.

The differences between the diminisher and the multiplier are as follows: the diminisher uses members' talents, while the multiplier develops them; the diminisher blames members for mistakes, while the multiplier encourages them to explore mistakes; the diminisher dictates the directions, while the multiplier challenges members to find directions; the diminisher makes decisions, while the multiplier consults them; and the diminisher controls the process, while the multiplier supports the members through the whole process.[14] Under the leadership of multipliers, members feel empowered and achieve more with limited resources.

Through an analysis of the data from their interviews, Wiseman found five disciplines. The first is the talent magnet, which attracts talented people and utilizes them at their highest points of contribution. It is essential to observe members and help them to bring their gifts and strengths for mission, rather than merely making a box and assigning people to it, resulting in an underuse of people's gift. The second is the liberator. The multiplier leader creates an intense environment that requires people's best thinking and work, rather than a tense one that suppresses people's thinking. When people find freedom to explore ideas, they will create and develop more ideas, including critical solutions. The third is the challenger, which helps members stretch their mind and evolve new ideas. The fourth is an open decision-making process, which emphasizes a freedom to disagree and requires vigorous debate and discussion. The leader here will need skill to facilitate debates in a contemplative way. The fifth is providing ownership for members, while avoiding micromanaging.[15]

The multipliers are the leaders who extract the members' best passion and who help them to be authentic. Of course, in the

---

14. Wiseman, *Multipliers*, 20.
15. Wiseman, *Multipliers*, 22–23.

shared leadership model, each member takes the role of leader, and, therefore, each one should be a multiplier.

Managing Uncertainty

In this ever-changing world of today, leaders should be comfortable with the unknown. When we face something that is unclear or unarticulated, leaders need to be able to navigate the path. For these moments, the key is to recognize the real value of the religious community.

Julie Benezet, a former leader at Amazon.com, mentions that "as a leader, you have to know who you are and for what you stand. You have to know your values, personal history, and dreams for the future. When living in a world of unknowns, knowing yourself gives you guiding lights, your core drivers to move you through the scariness of all the ambiguity that is your daily fare as a leader."[16] Maybe when we are faced with uncertainty, we should try to ask questions rather than giving answers. The questions themselves offer us a hint about where we are headed. Uncertainty is the reality. Every moment stands on some kind of an unknown, although human beings try to deny this truth. To face uncertainty means going to the mystery.

As a leader, one must face the reality of uncertainty in contemplation, which is a long and loving gaze at the real. To embrace uncertainty suggests living inside God's imagination, which is pluralistic, conflicted, disturbed, dynamic, and always on the way.[17] The leader who resides in God's imagination dares to dream in liminal space at a threshold moment.

Very often, we ask for a vision from the leader as a set of words. However, when a leader articulates something desirable, it is not a vision. A vision is a collective process that the community moves forward, while holding the dream; it is not just one person's ability to dream the future. Through mutual listening, the leader

16. Benezet, *Journey of Not Knowing*, 36.

17. Brueggemann, "Prophetic Imagination," 70.

can hold the vision, which comes from prayer, daily life struggles, laughter, discernment, and research. In other words, visions exist in the interstitial space where sisters encounter and share dreams and passions. Leaders hold any arising uncertainty comfortably, in trust of God and other members.

Also, the capacity to manage uncertainty comes from the ability to revisit the calling of the Jesus movement. In the Gospel of Matthew 28:10, the disciples are invited to go to Galilee, where they had first met Jesus. At the liminal moment of uncertainty between the passion and the resurrection, the disciples were afraid, confused, and disappointed. Just when they felt lost about God's imagination, they heard a voice saying, "Go to Galilee."

Pope Francis explained in a Holy Saturday homily, "to return to Galilee means *to re-read* everything—Jesus' preaching, his miracles, the new community, the excitement and the defections, even the betrayal—to re-read everything starting from the end, which is a new beginning, *from this supreme act of love.*" He continued to explain further as follows:

> In the life of every Christian, after baptism, there is also another Galilee, *a more existential* Galilee: the experience of a *personal encounter with Jesus Christ* who called me to follow him and to share in his mission. In this sense, returning to Galilee means treasuring in my heart the living memory of that call, when Jesus passed my way, gazed at us with mercy and asked me to follow him. To return there means reviving the memory of that moment when his eyes met mine, the moment when he made me realize that he loved me.[18]

Galilee is the space where the past of memory, the present of love, and the future of hope coexist. Returning to Galilee is the only way to hold uncertainty as a leader.

Furthermore, leaders should learn to manage uncertainty on the communal level. Uncertainty is not just a leader's lonely burden, but a tender yoke of sisterhood. In this way, there is neither a right vision nor a wrong one. There are only visions on the way,

18. Pope Francis, homily, Holy Saturday, April 19, 2014, para. 2.

as the process through which women religious experience sister-hood, generate greater consciousness, and deepen the call of mission in the global world. In shared leadership, all members—as leaders—hold one another for the vision becoming, where each member experiences spiritual transformation.

Networking

Religious in the twenty-first century may be smaller in numbers but we must be much more significant in vision and concern. The ethnic, national, and even congregational concerns will give place to the care and interest, on a global scale.[19] Then, networking emerges as an essential skill for leaders. Networking, by definition, suggests the exchange of information or services among individuals, groups, and institutions; networking enhances productivity. Networking also increasingly takes important roles in the global world, using technology as a process by which we develop mutually beneficial and long-term relationships with others.

As a way to delink the capital market system, which often ruins human dignity, networking can be utilized by activists as a tool to connect with global communities, as well as local groups, to promote justice and peace in the world. Women religious communities in the North have already begun to work with sisters who live in the Global South. Specific problems, such as human trafficking, will be more actively addressed when sisters work together globally in a structured manner, to break the loop of slavery, in which women are misplaced and dislocated.

In early Christianity, the network was one of the most crucial elements for rapid growth. The Greco-Roman urban setting was dense, and highly populated poor areas, called the *insular* or the apartment block, were the perfect environment to create a social knit. The poor in cities, who were severed from their family systems, were able to create a strong sense of community.[20] These

19. Harmer, *Religious Life in the 21st Century*, 100.
20 Billings, "From House Church to Tenement Church," 562.

converts found influential father/central figures such as Paul, who gave them a life orientation and, as a result, Christianity grew rapidly in the urban settings.

In this networking, the missionary or the itinerary preacher holds a vital role in creating a sense of community among the local church. Paul and his companions continued to maintain contact by writing letters and visiting. They consistently gave information and guidance, and encouraged them to support one another, spiritually as well as financially.

If we apply this networking model of early Christianity, we can create local community, sharing our calling and mission. At the same time, we must also continuously build networks by sharing information and creating common projects. For that, the leaders need to develop the keen skill of networking.

Networking requires commitment and discipline: set clear and well-defined goals for present networking activities; reconnect with people regularly; constantly follow up with people.[21] Networking on a global scale is cross-cultural and the leaders who create continuous networks are border crossers who act beyond their cultural comfort zones. Religious communities should teach cultural competency or, more accurately, teach cultural humility, not assuming any cultural norms but focusing on the mission, which comes from the call of the Jesus movement.

The leaders who commit to creating networks should understand their scope and goals. It is always challenging to follow up after networking. When connecting with other congregations, leaders should remember the missions or passions of the other communities, in dreaming about possibilities for collaborations with them. The leader must be skillful and dedicated to communication with her own community members, as well as with other communities.

Religious women in the twenty-first century stand in the light of a new reality that has emerged from the global community. In today's world, the ecological crisis and abject poverty grow more alarming, while global activism—which heavily accommodates

21. Bentson, *Focused Networking*, 59.

networking through the Internet, including the organization of gathering and the art of social critiquing—is emerging. It is time for women religious to open up to networking, through which we can learn, grow, and participate in social change. We do not have to teach the gospel value; in the world of networking, we can put out a voice and action of love and justice, which come directly from our vocation.

Encounters in Today's Reality: The Art of Bridge Building and Bridge Crossing[1]

TERE MAYA

> ahí está el puente
> para cruzarlo o para no cruzarlo
> yo lo voy a cruzar
> sin prevenciones
>
> —"El Puente" by Mario Benedetti

The present moment challenges us to witness the art of bridge building and bridge crossing. Religious women today are called to build all kinds of bridges: bridges between cultures and ways of thinking, bridges between ministries and organizations, bridges among religious congregations, and bridges between young and old. The pontificate of Pope Frances challenges us to build bridges. In fact, *pontiff* in Latin means "bridge builder." Over and over, Francis has been inviting the church to build bridges. To the young gathered in Poland for World Youth Day 2017, the pope said: "Become builders of bridges to break the logic of division, rejection, of fear of others, ensure your service to the poor."[2] For several years we have heard him affirm that Christians should

---

1. Portions of the chapter were presented at the Religious Formation Conference in 2017.

2. In the preface of a book in honor of St. Teresa of Calcutta, Pope Francis tells the young: "Sean constructores de puentes para romper la lógica de la división, del rechazo, del miedo de unos contra otros, pónganse al servicio de los pobres . . ." Pope Francis, "Homily."

build bridges, not walls. During the World Youth Day in Panama, again he spoke of bridges.[3]

Bridges great and small claim our imagination. The architectural and engineering genius that is required to create stable, flexible, and beautiful bridges is one of the highlights of human civilization. Throughout history, bridges of all kinds have created opportunities for encounter and relationship. Bridges have been at the heart of debates and wars for centuries. They have made it to the silver screen many times over and have been used as symbols of modernity and progress. Bridges have also sparked the imagination of musicians, poets, and painters.

Bridge building is an art. Bridges require engineering and precision, but also design, flexibility, and a lot of collaboration. Building bridges is also a dangerous task. I found in two children's poems the inspiration for the kind of bridge building that a culture of *encuentro* requires. An Argentinian writer, Elsa Isabel Bornemann, who challenged the dictatorship through her children's book, writes about drawing bridges.[4] Her poem "Puentes" ("Bridges") could serve as inspiration for the emerging mission for religious life:

> Yo dibujo puentes
> para que me encuentres
> Un puente de tela,
> con mis acuarelas. . .
> Un puente colgante,
> con tiza brillante. . .
> Puentes de madera,
> con lápiz de cera. . .
> Puentes levadizos,
> plateados, cobrizos. . .
> Puentes irrompibles,

3. During the World Youth Day in Panama 2019 he exhorted the Young: "Y este es un criterio para distinguir a la gente, los constructores de puentes y de muros, esos constructores de muros que dividen a la gente. ¿Ustedes qué quieren ser? ¡Constructores de puentes!" Pope Francis, "Discurso del Papa Francisco."

4. Bornemann's book *Un Elefante Ocupa Mucho Espacio* was banned during the Argentinian dictatorship.

de piedra, invisibles. . .
Y tú . . . ¡Quién creyera!
¡No los ves siquiera!
Hago cien, diez, uno. . .
¡No cruzas ninguno!
Mas . . . como te quiero. . .
dibujo y espero.
¡Bellos, bellos puentes
para que me encuentres!

I draw bridges
So you can find me
A bridge of cloth,
With my water color . . .
A hanging bridge,
With bright chalk . . .
A wooden bridge,
With my wooden pencil . . .
Draw bridges,
Silver, copper . . .
Unbreakable bridges,
Of stone, invisible ones.
And you . . . Who would have known!
¡You don't even see them!
I draw one hundred, ten, one.
¡You cross not one!
Yet . . . because I love you.
I draw and wait.
Beautiful, beautiful bridges
So you might find me![5]

We draw bridges, we create bridges because we love. That is
our mission. Our particular kind of bridge building requires collaboration and dialogue to kindle, nourish, build, encourage, foster,
unify. As Christians, and even more so as religious, we are required
to engage in the art of bridge building because we know that we
are called to the mission. Francis, in his exhortation *Gaudate et Ex-
sultate* ("Rejoice and Be Glad"), reminds us of that: "We are never

5. English translation by Tere Maya.

completely ourselves unless we belong to a people. That is why no one is saved alone, as an isolated individual. Rather God draws us to himself, taking into account the complex fabric of interpersonal relationships present in a human community."

Collaboration and dialogue are, therefore, essential attributes of the Christian life if we are to constantly strive to create unity as a human family made up of many peoples. Indeed, collaboration and dialogue create a community that humanizes our coexistence. Collaboration and dialogue create the possibility for transformation, where we discover that diversity is the intimate friend of unity. Only in an intentional, conscious effort to collaborate and dialogue with one another will we ever understand Jesus' prayer in John's Gospel: "That they may be one" (17:21).

Contemplation of the nature further urges us to the intentional, conscious effort to build communion through collaboration and dialogue. Scientists insist that we protect the fragile and beautiful ecosystems that shape our planet. *Laudato Sí* echoes this call by acknowledging that "it cannot be emphasized enough how everything is connected. Time and space are not independent of one another, and not even atoms or subatomic particles can be considered in isolation" (138). At a time when we are learning that even trees communicate with one another,[6] we absolutely must heed the lesson from nature that is begging humanity to evolve into greater collaboration.

The religious life that we see emerging has been shifting into this understanding of connection. Despite the "siloed" mentality that prevailed among and within religious institutes, sometimes accompanied by downright competition, religious are embracing the call to collaboration in so many different ways that a transformation will be unavoidable. Even though there are efforts toward collaboration that can be traced back several decades (those that gave shape to conferences like the LCWR and the Religious Formation Conference), today's collaboration bears a different significance. The self-sufficiency and often diplomatic collaboration of

---

6. Wohlleben's *The Hidden Life of Trees* has called our attention to the incredible connections that nature makes.

the earlier years around the council have given way to essential, even urgent collaborations.

As religious life continues to right-size, collaborative efforts will only increase and, in fact, will become the essential new normal. This might just be the most significant grace of our declining numbers in the United States. Congregations, large and small, that once needed no others are now leaning into collaborations even at the most basic levels. Gradually, this is also creating a new sacred space among us for hospitality. Just as we are welcoming the collaboration with other institutes, we are welcoming the collaboration with organizations that share our values for the common good, and we are welcoming conversations with other theologians, faith groups, and even non-believers. More and more, we are truly embracing what it means to be Catholic.

We are moving from an abstract understanding of Catholic as universal or inclusive into the heart of the Greek word *katha holos*. We are now "gathering in the whole." Our life, our ministries, our houses are becoming places where "all are welcome."[7] Gently, both because of need and conviction, we are creating new collaborations that are building bridges for the common good. Religious life is emerging as a life form of bridge builders!

Nevertheless, we must understand that building the bridge is not enough. At a talk I gave recently in Santa Clara, the audience reminded me that you can build bridges but not everyone crosses. True, I responded, but if there is no bridge, even fewer people will cross over. Here, I find inspiration in yet another children's poem. Shel Silverstein, American poet, cartoonist, and songwriter, wrote and illustrated the poem "The Bridge," where he warns:

> This bridge will only take you halfway there
> To those mysterious lands you long to see:
> Through gypsy camps and swirling Arab fairs
> And moonlit woods where unicorns run free.
> So come and walk awhile with me and share
> The twisting trails and wondrous worlds I've known.

7. Groom, *What Makes Us Catholic*, 127.

But this bridge will only take you halfway there—
The last few steps you'll have to take alone.[8]

As Silverstein says, we might build the bridges, but we cannot make anyone cross them. Yet this should not dissuade us from the critical task of bridging, because if the bridge is not there, then for sure no one will cross it! Furthermore, a well-made bridge always entices one to cross. That is why Mario Benedetti's poem is a response to Shel Silverstein: "There is the bridge, to be crossed or not be crossed, I will cross with without hesitation!" Building bridges cannot be a choice for us, but crossing always is. The future of humanity demands new architects that will create the bridges to save us and our planet. We find bridge building and collaboration is one of the most hope-filled traits of the religious life that is emerging in the United States. The architects, engineers, and artists that will create the bridges to gather us into a people in unity have been born, and they are already at work among us.

The Culture of Encounter: The Resistance of Tribalism

The times we live in require that we join the resistance. Like the freedom fighters of many critical moments in human history, we find men and women religious who have joined the resistance. They are resisting the growing "phobias" that are challenging our common humanity: the fear of the "other" that separates, alienates, discriminates, ostracizes, marginalizes and denigrates; and the "tribalism"— understood as a distortion of tribal identity—that continues to grow in our North American environments. Accepting difference and respecting diversity need not lead to exclusion and segregation. In fact, the more we trend away from a culture that embraces diversity, respect, and tolerance, the more likely that the fear and tribalism will only grow stronger and more dangerous.

Our goal as religious needs to be the modeling of intercultural living. Anthony Gittins explains that intercultural living is

8. Silverstein "This Bridge," 168.

a faith-based proposition that has to become integral to our understanding of religious life.[9] The good news is that this respect for diversity, this positive thriving in diversity, more and more characterizes the relationships and friendships of our younger religious. They are developing a kinship for one another in the midst of their diversity that will quite simply transform our understanding of religious life. But first, let us consider the tribalism they are up against.

Ideological tribes are pervasive and sometimes downright dangerous. Fueled by mass communication and especially social media, they polarize and divide. Without bridges and bridge crossers, we will soon find ourselves in ideological camps walled from outside thinking and from anyone who is different. The language of judgment and condemnation has characterized the modern brand of religious tribalism, but the level of hatred, violence, and dehumanization that they are now spewing chills my heart. There is no way—absolutely no way—that Jesus would recognize this language of hate and division in some of the current-day digital religious tribes. When compassion and mercy are not part of the vocabulary, we must know we have encountered a Christian heresy. Faith leaders across the United States have organized to warn of this distortion of Jesus's message. The "Reclaiming Jesus: Speaking Up for the Integrity of Our Faith" movement challenges us to reclaim the integrity of the gospel message, where all are welcome![10] Catholic men and women religious, sadly, are found in some of these "tribes"; if religious life is to live into its calling, it must absolutely resist the temptation of tribalism. Authentic discernment must call us into awareness, a level of critical thinking that always places compassion over judgment.

Another form of tribalism that needs to be resisted is xenophobia. If we seek to live in a culture of encounter we cannot live in a century of massive human mobility thinking that walls and policing will suddenly damper the massive arrival of refugees and

9. Gittins, *Living Mission Interculturally*, 4.

10. Faith leaders have issued a "Confession of Faith in a Time of Crisis," para. 6.

migrants. Even as our migration debates continue, new maps are being drawn across the globe. Regions are emerging that demand a remapping, a new understanding of place and demography.

A culture of encounter needs to engage with this massive human migration. Certainly, we must all collaborate so that people can experience human dignity through access to a livelihood, respect for human rights, and protection from harm. Religious around the world should be especially collaborating so that the dreadful situations that force so many refugees out of their homes are no longer the cause for human migration. We are called to globalized solidarity that can move beyond the politically motivated aid that so harmed so many parts of the global south, that can respect local customs and culture, and that can be done in respectful mutuality.

Bridging Encounters in Today's Reality

A culture of encounter requires placement. We first need to understand the "place" we serve in as men and women religious. We need to situate ourselves clearly before we can answer the call to encounter. As religious serving in the United States, we need to recognize not just the significance of the place we have been called to live this life, but also what this means for the rest of the church and the world. For a long time, we have realized that we serve in a country where anything that happens politically or economically sends ripples throughout the world. For example, in Mexico they say that when the US gets a cold, Mexico gets pneumonia.

Are we fully aware of the time and place that we are called to live in—the context of our call to *encuentro*? Do we have our feet "placed" firmly in this "place" and in this "time" we have been called to serve in? *Encuentro*, indeed the incarnation, always happens in a particular time and place. The encounters with Jesus in the Gospels are often described in detail concerning the time of day or the place. Jesus encounters the Samaritan at the well, and the first disciples followed Jesus "in the afternoon." Encounters happen in real time, in real places. The natural disasters that have surrounded us bring this painfully to mind. The hours we spent tracking hurricanes and fires, the pictures of places familiar to our communities in Texas, Florida, Puerto Rico, the US Virgin Islands, and Northern California remind us that this is the place where our mission is to create a culture of encounter.

We have been called to encourage a culture of *encuentro* in North America today. We live in a place with striking similarity to Palestine in the time of Jesus. The parallels should not be ignored. Today the United States is a crossroads for the world—of ideas, people, goods, and services. Despite changes around the world, the US continues to be the top destination for migrants around the world.[11] The Catholic Church in the United States is quickly becoming the most diverse local church in the world. The United States Conference of Catholic Bishops' Office for Cultural Diversity in the Church explains, "The Catholic Church in the United States is one of the most culturally diverse institutions in the country and it will become even more diverse in the future."[12] Formation for a culture of encounter needs to assume this "placement" fully. When our communities sent missionaries abroad, we were very intentional about the inculturation of the gospel, about culturally sensitive training, about language learning. We participated in programs like Maryknoll and MACC. Today we need equivalent programs to serve locally. Our cities, parishes, and neighborhoods are very diverse. In addition, we need to ask ourselves if our initial and ongoing formation programs have shifted in the same way as the identity of our local churches has. Our charisms are called to encounter the people we serve—and this we do in an ever-changing landscape of diversity—of every kind, not just cultural or ethnic. The prophetic call of our life demands that our communities stand in this place of all diversities and be witness to the radical hospitality of the gospel.

The call to create a culture of encounter happens in this place in a very particular time. Our time requires courageous engagement. The temptation to stay "inside"—our communities, our ministries,

---

11. "Global Migration Trends Factsheet," paras. 1–17.

12. USCCB, "New Study On Cultural Diversity," para. 6.

our own aging—endangers our charism. The Latin American bishops gathered in Aparecida in 2007 and expressed *encuentro* in one of the most beautiful documents they have published. To understand *Evangelii Gaudium* deeply, we need to read *Aparecida*, a document little discussed in the United States. The Latin American bishops wrote their conclusion as follows:

> We cannot let this hour of grace slip by. We need a new Pentecost! We need to go out to meet individuals, families, communities, and peoples to communicate to them, and share the gift of encounter with Christ, who has filled our lives with "meaning," truth and love, joy and hope! We cannot passively and calmly wait in our church buildings, but we must move out in all directions to proclaim that evil and death do not have the last word, that love is stronger, that we have been liberated and saved by the Lord's paschal victory in history, that He calls us into Church, and wants to multiply the number of his disciples and missionaries in building his Kingdom in our continent. We are witnesses and missionaries: in large cities and the countryside, in the mountains and jungles of our Americas, in all the areas of shared social life, in the most varied "Aeropagus" settings of the public life of nations, in the extreme situations of existence, assuming ad gentes our concern for the Church's universal mission.[13]

Evangelii Gaudium almost echoes this call. Pope Francis is calling us at this time to "go forth," to "go out," "una Iglesia en salida." We are called to engage with our time in constant motion toward the other in a constant dynamic of encounter. The time we have been called to live our call to community in our charism is different. Our communities are charged to bridge the present and the future by living fully in our present. Only the intentional commitment to a culture of encounter in this time and this place will ensure we are prophetically faithful to the gospel today.

---

13. *Concluding Document: Aparecida*, 458.

Encounter a "Continental" Tradition

Encuentro is happening everywhere. But we have been also called to a formal appointment with *encuentro* by our own church in the United States. The V National Encuentro is now in its implementation process. We know as church we are called to an *encuentro* with our Latino brothers and sisters to "to discern ways in which the Church in the United States can better respond to the Hispanic/Latino presence and to strengthen the ways in which Hispanics/Latinos respond to the call to the New Evangelization as missionary disciples serving the entire Church."[14] It is no coincidence that the process is called an *encuentro*. Long before Pope Francis wrote about it, our Latino Catholic community has been gathering in national *encuentros*. Many members of our communities have been going to *encuentros* since 1972. This is a forty-five-year history of *encuentro*—right here in the United States.[15] Perhaps it is time for our communities as a whole to notice what this *encuentro* is claiming from us as religious in the United States and to embrace this contribution, this gift, from our Latino communities, to make their gift of *encuentro* ours. In fact, we need to embrace our "continental belonging"—our being part of the Americas—and also honor the Latin American contribution to *encuentro*, a long tradition that comes from the idea of "pastoral de conjunto," a community pastoral approach, that is at the heart of the national *encuentros*.[16]

Moreover, I would suggest that we even need to enter into the bilingual gift our Latino brothers and sisters bring to the understanding of *encuentro*. I think we need to turn to Spanish to notice the depth in the meaning of a culture of *encuentro*. The word *encuentro* is related to so many others, *encontrarse*—"to get together"; *encuentro*—as a gathering or meeting, even a conference; *encuentro*—as butting heads, or having a conflict; *encuentro*—as sports match; or re-*encuentro*—a second meeting; and there is more: *econtronazo*—a crash; *llevarse al encuentro*—"drag along";

14. https://vencuentro.org, "What is the Goal of the V Encuentro?"

15. USCCB, "History of Hispanic Ministry," paras. 3–4.

16. Matovina, *Latino Catholicism*, 86.

or *desecuentro*—a failed meeting or conversation. *Encuentro* has so many levels of meaning that the Spanish reminds us that it is a fluid term, understood in context, and even better understood in practice. You know if there has been a true *encuentro*—only after you are finished.

This placement in time also requires an awareness that our communities are called to an understanding of the church that transcends the geopolitical boundaries that sometimes confine us. Nearly twenty years ago, St. John Paul II gathered the bishops of the American continent—of all the Americas. His dream of a church of the Americas, a Pan-American church, was finally expressed in this synod, Ecclesia in America:

> The Church in America is called not only to promote greater integration between nations, thus helping to create an authentic globalized culture of solidarity, but also to cooperate with every legitimate means in reducing the negative effects of globalization, such as the domination of the powerful over the weak, especially in the economic sphere, and the loss of the values of local cultures in favor of a misconstrued homogenization.[17]

The bishops' conferences have been meeting—not always with the same passion as when they gathered in the synod, but still, they meet. Moreover, our own conferences of religious have been gathering with our Canadian and Latin American counterparts for years even well before the Synod on the Americas. The flow of missionaries and ideas over the years has slowly been weaving a region that recognizes how porous borders really are! Today, all this time later, we may finally be living into this dream.

Religious life will play a critical role in the region provided it can recognize both its gift and its unique call in this new continental reality. Many of our congregations have been reconfiguring by regions in the Americas. The Caribbean, Mexico, and Canada appear from the distance of *Roman Generalates* and from many of our local governance structures like logical geographical regions. I guess it's easier from far away. For years, we have been involved

17. John Paul II, *Ecclesia in America*, 55.

in Central and South America. Many of our communities have strong relationships in these areas and are currently reconfiguring. The number of North American religious congregations with ministries or units in South America is significant, which requires a reflection about our internal "culture of *encuentro*." These include the Mercy's, the Sisters of Providence, Oblates, Missionaries of the Sacred Heart, IHMs, CCVIs. Our presence in Latin America has changed our communities and will continue to do so. Because of this experience, we are natural ministers in our US church. We understand the language and culture; we have learned to live into the encounter. For this reason, we know we need to restructure our formation programs so that we are ready for even closer encounters. The mission is coming home to North America.

Knowingly or not, we are already being transformed by this continental identity. We serve in the continent where most migrants move, we serve the local church that welcomes most of them, and we serve in communities of religious that are increasingly diverse. Encounter is the air we breathe; it happens all the time around us. However, for these encounters to be transformed by the gospel to create a "gospel of encounter"—a good news of encounter or hospitality, and intercultural learning—we need to be intentional. Anthony Gittins reminds us that unless we meet the challenge of intercultural living, communities will face fragmentation of community and the inability to serve the mission.[18]

We need a new formation for this new mindset. The evolving concept of *mestizaje* may well embrace this call for intercultural living for our American continent. Our own prophet, Virgil Elizondo, wrote the "future is *Mestizo*."[19] Latino/a theologians in the US have since taken this reflection and explored it further.[20] Virgil's insight into how an encounter of cultures creates a new *mestizaje* echoes what Anthony Gittins has been writing about intercultural living. The measure of an authentic culture of encounter is the level of

18. See Gittins, *Living Mission Interculturally.*

19. See Elizondo, *Future Is Mestizo.*

20. Aquino "Two Tropes of Mestizaje," 285.

mestizaje or intercultural transformation that results from ongoing intentional encounter. And we live in the continent of *mestizaje*! Throughout history and in the midst of contradictions, mestizo culture, which is the most widespread among many peoples in the region, has sought to combine these multiple original cultural sources, facilitating the dialogue of their respective worldviews and enabling them to converge into a shared history. To this cultural complexity would also have to be added that of the many European immigrants who settled in the countries of our region. We may fall into the temptation of a "nativist" agenda, and we may quietly lament the times of mono-cultural ministry, where things were simple and all in one language. But we were not called to live at that place in that time; we are called to live in the present, in the never-ending encounter with all diversity. Our religious brothers and sisters are living into this commitment. The CLAR, Latin-American Conference of Religious, in one of their assemblies opted for a "culture of *encuentro*" and chose the icon of the visitation. Holy Spirit Sister Mercedes Casas, currently serving as president, challenged men and women religious in Latin America:

> Our world, our Caribbean and Latin American countries, our families and our religious congregations need the Visitation. We need a Consecrated Life with initiative, not afraid to leave its security and go out to live a real solidarity. We need a Consecrated Life alert to the necessities of others and alive to vitality both within itself and wherever else it is flowering or has potential to flower. We need a Consecrated Life in touch with the earth and devoted to taking care of our common home.[21]

Latin American religious have been challenged to a "dynamic culture of *Encuentro*, the fruit and the impulse of new dynamics of relationships that need to weave through all the assumed commitments and that give a humanizing impulse to our communities in a missionary going forth."[22]

21. Sánchez, "Introduction—Inspirational Guidelines," para. 2.

22. See "Horizonte Inspirador de la Vida Consagrada en América Latina y el Caribe," para. 5.

The Latin-American church has been about *encuentro* for a while now. The national *encuentros* in the United States have brought this gift to the northern part of the continent. To understand the call to create a culture of *encuentro*, we need to turn to the church that gave us our current pope. Several authors have already called our attention to Latin America. Allan Deck explains, "The profound Latin American experience of this pope, especially his highly successful participation in the pastoral reflection, planning, and writing projects of CELAM . . . is a fundamental source of inspiration and guidance for him."[23] It was *Aparecida* that highlighted our call to be *discipulos-misioneros*. I use the Spanish because the conference claimed that first you need to be a follower before you can be a missionary. English flips this and we say "missionary disciples," which is why we need to be bilingual to ensure that both are in constant motion! "Missionary disciples, missionary disciples" and on and on: "Here lies the fundamental challenge that we face: to show the church's capacity to promote and form disciples and missionaries who respond to the calling received and to communicate everywhere, in an outpouring of gratitude and joy, the gift of the encounter with Jesus Christ."[24]

The *Encuentro* with Jesus Christ

The other-centeredness nature of the culture of *encuentro* begins in the personal encounter with Jesus but never ends there. The proof of authentic *encuentro* continues to be the love of neighbor. We know that we have had an authentic encounter with Jesus when we continue to move toward the encounter with those around us. In fact, the call to *encuentro* is also a call to a journey beyond ourselves, beyond our comfort, a renewed journey to the margins.

This call to encounter Christ is rooted in the community gathered for Eucharist. A fresh and renewed commitment to the Eucharistic *encuentro* is essential to the culture of encounter that

23. Deck, *Francis: Bishop of Rome*, 4.
24. *Concluding Document: Aparecida*, 14.

grounds our being as religious. *Aparecida* affirms we are a people called to be sent: "The Eucharist is the privileged place of the disciple's encounter with Jesus Christ. With this sacrament, Jesus attracts us to himself and makes us enter into his dynamism toward God and toward neighbor."[25]

The encounter with Jesus Christ in the poor is a constitutive dimension of our faith in Jesus Christ. Our option emerges from contemplation of his suffering face in them and from the encounter with him in the afflicted and outcast, whose immense dignity he himself reveals to us. It is our very adherence to Jesus Christ that makes us friends of the poor and unites us to their fate.[26] The meaning of a culture of *encuentro* is found in the movement from the one to the whole. We must encounter each other, we must encounter Jesus Christ, and we are called to encounter those in the margins.

Pope Francis may indeed be one of the most significant voices calling for *encuentro*. But Pope Benedict before him, in the encyclical *Deus Caritas Est* ("God Is Love"), called us to a full awareness that an encounter is at the core of the Christian call: "Being Christian is not the result of an ethical choice or a lofty idea, but the encounter with an event, a person, which gives life a new horizon and a decisive direction" (*Deus Caritas Est*, 1). Pope Benedict reminded us in many ways that to understand a culture of encounter *we must first cultivate our encounter with Jesus Christ.*[27] The fundamental meeting is at the heart of the culture of encounter—our encountering Jesus Christ. As obvious and basic as this sounds, we need to ask ourselves as religious in what ways the encounter with Jesus is the golden thread of our formation programs.

To understand the heart of the culture of encounter, we need to enter deeply into our daily and communal encounter with Jesus. The one thing, the one message Francis insists on, the encounter with Jesus, is always clear. *Evangelii Gaudium* ("The Joy of the Gospel"), an apostolic exhortation in 2013, begins with it: "I invite

---

25. *Concluding Document: Aparecida*, 251.

26. *Concluding Document: Aparecida*, 257.

27. One of Pope Benedict XVI's major works was the three-volume *Jesus of Nazareth*.

all Christians, everywhere, at this very moment, to a renewed personal encounter with Jesus Christ, or at least an openness to letting him encounter them; I ask all of you to do this unfailingly each day" (*Evangelii Gaudium*, 3). Pope Francis constantly returns to this encounter: "This is today's message: Jesus' encounter with his people; the encounter of Jesus who serves, who helps, who is the servant, who lowers himself, who is compassionate with all those in need."[28] Contemplating Jesus' capacity for encounter with the poor, the marginalized, women, children, and people from other cultures opens up possibilities for ourselves.

A Community of *Encuentro*

A culture of *encuentro* needs community. We know it; we struggle with it. We even talk about "intentional community." My intention is simply to point out a few traits of a community of *encuentro*. Community needs a place. I think we often underestimate the "ecosystem" in which we are called to community and *encuentro*. When reflecting on community, I am reminded once again of my community park, a place of harmony, respect, relationship, joy, serenity, and, yes, fun and welcome. I believe that nature itself is clamoring for a deeper understanding of community that includes all of creation. Perhaps we need to read *Laudato Si* as a blueprint for human community. When speaking about the lack of harmony experience in extreme poverty, Francis insists that love always proves more powerful. Many people in these conditions are able to weave bonds of belonging and togetherness, which convert overcrowding into an experience of community in which the walls of the ego are torn down and the barriers of selfishness overcome. This experience of a communitarian salvation often generates creative ideas for the improvement of a building or a neighborhood (*Laudato Si*, 149).

An *encuentro* community needs to be a place like the park I love to visit, where people from all over come and gather, a place

28. Pope Francis, "For a Culture of Encounter," para. 7.

where we weave bonds of belonging and togetherness. The culture of *encuentro* is a culture that weaves relationship, one moment at a time, one strand at a time, in the particular time and place we are called to live in. Being in community with the intentional effort of weaving a culture of *encuentro* creates other possibilities. This communion becomes a place for imagination and creativity.

In fact, Chilean biologist Humberto Maturana spoke of the social implications of the *process of autopoiesis* or self-creation. He argued that living beings are cyclical, dynamic systems with networks of self-production made up of the molecular components, and with time he recognized that biology was also a social interaction. Maturana eventually spoke of humans as beings that are both biological and cultural, or biocultural, as he liked to say, since both realities are indivisible.[29] I bring up a Chilean biologist's insight because it was the groundwork for systems thinking, especially ecosystems, and our religious communities need to become healthy ecosystems that can self-reproduce if we are to remain faithful to our call to witness to the gospel. And to become healthy ecosystems we need a consistent and deeply rooted culture of *encuentro*.

This culture of *encuentro* needs nourishment and encouragement; it does not happen automatically but is the result of hard work. Anthony Gittins suggests that "goodwill is surely very necessary, but alone it remains quite insufficient. Also required are commitment and the sustained hard work necessary."[30] Dr. David Suzuki, following the work of Maturana and other ecologists, argued, "From microscopic genes to large-scale biological systems, and from natural ecosystems to human communities, diversity brings strength and resilience in the face of ever-changing conditions."[31] We have come to believe that diversity is critical for survival. The Universal Declaration on Cultural Diversity affirms this to be true:

---

29. Cossio, "40 Años de la Autopoiesis de Maturana," para. 1.
30. Gittins, *Living Mission Interculturally*, 5.
31. Suzuki, "Diversity Is Key to Survival," para. 4.

Culture takes diverse forms across time and space. This diversity is embodied in the uniqueness and plurality of the identities of the groups and societies making up humankind. As a source of exchange, innovation, and creativity, cultural diversity is as necessary for humankind as biodiversity is for nature. In this sense, it is the common heritage of humanity and should be recognized and affirmed for the benefit of present and future generations.[32]

However, diversity without a culture of *encuentro* is unlivable. Community, diversity, the very survival of the hope of gospel life embodied in our charisms happen when we live *encuentro*. Community, in fact, is created through the ongoing process of *encuentro*. A community of encounter in diversity becomes the place of gospel life we are all called to. The grace we need first of all is to recognize that this is the community that is required of us at this time; that to create places of healthy *encuentro* in diversity, places hospitable to *encuentro*, is already one of the most important things that is "ours to do at this time, in this place." To witness to the human capacity not only to tolerate each other but also to live with each other and to self-create systems with a healthy culture of *encuentro* may very well heal our broken and fragmented world. I borrow Pope Benedict's words:

> What does faith in this God give us? The first response is: it gives us a family, the universal family of God in the Catholic Church. Faith releases us from the isolation of the "I", because it leads us to communion: the encounter with God is, in itself and as such, an encounter with our brothers and sisters, an act of convocation, of unification, of responsibility towards the other and towards others. In this sense, the preferential option for the poor is implicit in the Christological faith in the God who became poor for us, so as to enrich us with his poverty (cf. 2 Cor 8:9).[33]

32. UNESCO, "Universal Declaration on Cultural Diversity," para. 1.
33. Pope Benedict XVI, *Aparecida*, 6–7.

The grace of *encuentro* calls us to re-create our communities. We first must gather, but we then need to move beyond creating places of mere "tolerance" to creating intercultural living spaces where daily encounters transform our diversities into healthy ecosystems—a daunting and ambitious task, but imperative to the time we live in.

Naming the *Desencuentro*

We are well aware of the call. The time and place we have been called to live our call to religious life requires a singular commitment to building and sustaining (cultivating) a culture of *encuentro*. Our communities will be those places if we can name and work through all the *desencuentros*, or the "non-*encuentros*" that find their way into our daily living of our charism, our ministry, and our interactions. We need to claim the *encuentro* and *desencuentro* that has grown together like the wheat and the weed. We must discern the difference. The time has come to tell them apart. We need to claim all the diversities that have been part of our communities, even those we were taught to forget or leave behind—and we need to claim the absence of diversity. Embracing both will help us live into the call of a culture of encounter. Encounter happens in the midst of a "diversity paradox," as Jacob Jenkins describes it.

We use diversity lightly, often narrowing down the dynamic complexity it involves. Diversity is an ever-changing reality that works in the here and now. To embrace the call to *Encuentro*, we must also note that it happens in the measure that we are capable to discern the diversity that surrounds us, that represents and confronts us. We must notice the diversities beyond the obvious ones, like culture and ethnicity, and notice the complicated ones like gender, age, able-bodiedness, economy, religion, language, region, theology, and many others. Failure to notice, to embrace the different diversities that we are called to encounter can result in a *desencuentro* because it will displace religious life from the place it has been called to.

115

Another *desencuentro* is found in the failure to assume our own history. Religious Life in the United States needs to revisit its own history, both to recognize its *encuentro* moments and its *desencuentro* moments. We need to recognize our communities are the result of the single-minded purpose to become one, the assimilation paradigm that undergirded most of our formation. Acculturation and uniformity kept us from tapping fully into the wealth of all the different kinds of diversities that have been part of our history.[34] Such diversities include the immigrant religious, the regional diversity, even the generational diversities, not to mention giftedness and point of view. Surely, we were not as racially diverse as we are becoming now, but that does not mean other diversities were not part of our DNA. We need to reconcile our own history of *desencuentro* before we can live fully into a culture of *Encuentro*.

Finally, we need to understand the *desencuentros* that are part of our time and place. We are not exempt from their complexity and their challenge. The culture of encounter that is required of us needs an honest and loving look at the *desencuentros* that surround us. The lack of civil discourse conspires against the very basic call to relationship that is the first step toward a culture of *encuentro*. The racism that lies at the root of so many of the injustices of our time and creeps its way into our communities, our ministries, and our worldviews require breaking the silence that has been part of our history. Bryan Massingale challenges us rightly:

> Racism is one of the central human rights challenges facing the country; it is the subtext of almost every social concern in our nation. It is my conviction—one that has only grown stronger with sustained study and reflection—that "Catholic failure to engage adequately the pivotal issue of racial injustice decisively compromises its theology of justice and renders its praxis of justice ineffective."[35]

Our complicity in systems of exclusion requires a process of reconciliation that will make our engagement with a culture

34. Gittins, *Living Mission Interculturally*, 6.
35. Massingale, *Racial Justice*, 9.

of *encuentro* authentic. This may well model a new way of being together in a society increasingly polarized and intent on separation and distance.

Encuentro as the Grace of Moment

We always have a choice on how we behold the unfolding future. We can lament what is passing and remain stuck in the diminishment narrative that has been divisive and disillusioning, or we can begin to see every bridge and every *encuentro* as the grace God is calling us into. That religious life will be smaller is a reality that must be embraced with joy. Perhaps, just perhaps, God is making something new in the midst of all the grief of rightsizing! Perhaps, just perhaps, this newness is in the hearts of the younger and more diverse religious who are joining our communities. And perhaps, this newness is all about *encuentro* as bridge building. I believe that it is.

In the end, building bridges will bring us all peace. We will have responded to the call when we have built all kinds of bridges. We will see elder sisters and younger sisters cross them. We will witness the encounters that crossing will allow. We will see that religious life has a remarkable capacity to tear down walls: the walls of the past, the walls of prejudice, the walls of resentment, the walls of ideology. We will believe that in the years to come we will create communities that witness to encounter. Slowly, we will build a bridge to the future to which God is calling all of religious life.

We will build bridges, temporary and permanent. We will build bridges with structures and programs. We will build bridges among us for dialogue and encounter. And we will invite the people of God to cross them with courage and faith. The future awaits!

Conclusion

(In my sleep I dreamed this poem)

Someone I loved once gave me
a box full of darkness.

It took me years to understand
that this, too, was a gift.

—"The Uses of Sorrow" by Mary Oliver

5 AM: the frogs
Asks what is it, what is it?
It is what it is.

— "5 AM" by Campbell McGrath

A re we, apostolic women religious who have taken crucial roles in fostering justice and peace, disappearing along with many beautiful living creatures, or are we being transformed in a new way? Honestly, when I began this book project, I did not have full confidence in the future, fully embracing sorrow and doubt. But I dreamed strongly and hoped. At the dawn of the twenty-first century, we are sincerely asking what religious life is, and particularly what apostolic religious life is. After searching for an answer, I can now generally describe what it is, but there is a process yet to come to reach a full answer. Maybe we are tempted to see the future, and so we are not focused on the present. In my New Testament class, my students and I are constantly surprised by the apocalyptic vision of Paul to stand firm in the present moment. If we can add onto that, it would be to "stay in the present moment, focused on the calling by Jesus to seek love," and this phrase has stayed with me more and more strongly over time.

For me, the writing of this book became a process—of reaching the reference point of religious life as it is emerging and to face religious life as it is, feeling neither threatened nor frustrated. Of course, I neither try to give direction nor exhortation for the future in this book. Rather, this is a reflection on the present moment, in which the past and the future exist simultaneously.

I have lost many sisters who were my mentors, wisdom figures, and model sisters. Recent Vatican statistics say that women religious have decreased every year by 1.6 percent.[1] As a woman religious admitting the frustration and sadness that I have faced in my journey, I can now confess feeling comfortable in being few; I even see it as a spiritual gift. By struggling with this uncomfortable yet compelling topic on emerging religious life in the twenty-first century, we can glimpse where we are located, as well as where we are going.

Even when I have felt lost and inundated with ministerial work, I have always been able to find the desire to continue this journey with love, holding hope for the future. When I encounter and converse with other women religious at the well, I feel revitalized, just as Jesus and the Samaritan woman did. Although I have no bucket to even draw water in today's uncertain world, I feel comforted and confident enough to serve the world with other women religious around the globe.

During my research of religious life and other critical thoughts applicable to religious life in the twenty-first century, especially my two-year dialogue with Sr. Tere Maya and with other sisters and young men and women, I have been gifted with sincere companionships with many who dream of the future. This writing process has provided me with a new lens through which to comprehend the religious life that has been given to me as a gift.

At the liminal space, as the in-between space, I have found common concerns and passion for religious life awaiting the dawn of hope for religious life and fostering a space of encounter.

1. Glatz, "Number of Priest Declined," para. 1.

We all have different working styles, schedules, and cultures, and the differences have served as a nest for creative collaboration, which we understand as the virtue of religious life. This book project has given me a sense of hope for our future, focused on collaboration and networking. Remaining in frequent and constant dialogue with our acquaintances should become our spiritual discipline. The writing of this book is mainly my own work and all responsibilities corresponding to it belong to me, but many of the insights and creative ideas emerged through dialogue with numerous women religious.

This book is my sharing with readers the gifts I have received through dialogues and personal struggles. Because this book is a type of tapestry, readers will find dissonance, distinctions, and repetition as ways of negating the universalized one-dimensional notion of religious life. I have tried to dialogically convey explorations of new ways of religious life in the US and around the globe. Religious life in the twenty-first century can be understood as existing in interstitial space through an interaction of four arenas.

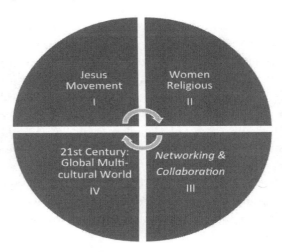

Fig. 2. Religious Life in the Twenty-First Century

The apostolic religious life can be understood as a movement that originates from Jesus, who proclaims the kingdom of heaven on earth. Arena I is the foundation and summit of the presence and activity of women religious. Whenever we feel confused or distressed, it is important that we return to arena 1. For me, the space of this arena signifies Galilee, where Jesus promised to his disciples. In the twenty-first century, Galilee could be the desert, a metropolitan inner city, or the exile space. However, it is clear that in Galilee women religious can renew their calling and regain a vision for their mission. There are various groups of people at work, and our distinction from those others is the fact that women religious are part of the Jesus movement.

The Jesus movement emerged in first-century Judea, where a marginal group in the Roman Empire challenged people and operated as a driving force to transform the world. Now in the twenty-first century, it is easy to find various forms of social activism that bring about justice and peace. Here we need to learn from others and deepen our commitment to bring on the kingdom of heaven. We need to nurture our unique position as women religious, which comes from our vocation and calling.

Sociopolitically, I situate contemporary religious life—and this discourse on it—in a world where social order is controlled by a global market system that aims to create more capital by exploiting resources. In this frame, arena IV is the global world, but, at the same time, it is the world God loves so much in which an alternative vision can come true. In this world, in the midst of global mobility, many different people encounter each other unexpectedly, and many sisters and lay men and women together imagine a possibility of creating a new world. Thus, arenas I, II, and IV constantly and simultaneously influence each other.

Arena III, then, manifests how we build the Kingdom Of Heaven in this global world. The networking and collaborations signify a method, but they may not directly be related to the outcome or product. However, what is most important is movement and interaction. As long as people encounter, engage, and live interculturally, life itself will be prophetic, and small steps will create a certain voice for the world.

Thus, women religious in arena II function as subjects in the Jesus movement, in which they manifest the values of the gospel in explicit opposition to the values of the world. In this global and multicultural world, each religious must understand intercultural living as a prophetic action countering the cultural and racial biases against people of color. Rather, each religious should—by encountering various ways of otherness—create a hybrid identity, through which one can embrace plural ways and negate all single norms. Through cultural humility, religious communities can learn how to embody gospel values.

Women religious communities fully understand the beauty of smallness, whose merits can be delineated as being intimate, diverse, and sustainable. In a small size, each member is able to practice a leadership role which is based on humanity—not perfect but vulnerable. Here, mutual learning and sharing is emphasized, rather than heroism.

The capacity to embrace ministry will parallel our capacity for networking and collaboration, as well as the spiritual maturity to admit weakness and the openness to learning from others. Here, the privilege of women religious is not authority, but the enjoyment of being sisters to other sisters and other people. Women religious have no official position in the institutional church, but we stand as a free prophetic voice. The Jesus movement stands as a paradox—a foolish *raison d'être*. The mission of religious women claims the foolishness of the cross, and, as such, the movement is never efficient or always successful. Rather, the power of vocation paradoxically stands in inefficiency and, often, loss. Peter worked all night, but could not catch a single fish (Luke 5). Then Jesus invited Peter to go deep. Religious life is a vocation of going deep. We are those who boast about the foolishness of the cross, which means we are looking for the treasures of heaven among the poor. We even enjoy failure in this endeavor. The Japanese Catholic writer Endo Shusaku, in the book *Wonderful Fool*, describes a missionary man who is innocent and unsuccessful, yet is able to transform other people.

Then, we can consider the process of facing the new reality of religious life in today's world. The first step is to remap our social location in order to dialogue with the current reality, which we discussed in this book: a multicultural, border-crossing, and global world. When we talk about being multicultural, we must keep in mind that there are many people who experience dislocation and immigration, with or without legal status, and we engage with those who experience being in new lands. Pope Francis emphasizes that we should not be afraid of exiles and immigrants, but rather we should try to encounter them. For a better life, people often cross borders and, as a consequence, create multicultural societies. While multiculturalism pays attention to diversity and difference, the term *border crossing* emphasizes any action that encounters an unfamiliar other. Here, encounter brings a great sense of fear and discomfort, yet it can also transform us. In the poetic action of encounter through the practice of hospitality, people can create various hybrid identities. The new personality—called hybridity—will never be the same as before and will bring mutual transformation.

Also, this world we live in is a globalized one. The characterization of globalization is communication, technology, and a free-market system, which often go together, so that many people enjoy a great level of mobility and social media connections. We can know what is going on in the world easily, but not everyone has access.

Because this global world is operated by a free-market system, people who are left out from the pool of capitalism can fall into deep poverty. Many countries suffer from debt, and people without technology or education can easily become homeless or dislocated. Any crime against human rights can become larger due to this global scale. For example, human trafficking is not just a local problem and must be considered globally and through various perspectives, such as gender, sexuality, poverty, and technology.

The border-crossing action or being a border crosser implicates two meanings of geography and spirituality, which often intersect. We in the global world cross borders frequently. If we enter other countries through a border crossing, we can feel weird and confused. Such a space is a non-space, in which we have left behind our own culture but have not yet arrived at a new, unknown culture.

The more we cross borders, the more we should learn about cultural humility, with which we understand our own cultural norms and how to live interculturally. Holding back one's assumptions and listening to others is an action of border crossing. Horticulture shows that a mixed soil is always more fertile; diversity always brings more life and fruits.

The second step is be aware of the limits and possibilities of women religious. It is obvious that we are becoming fewer and older. The cohort that comprises 80 percent of women religious in the US is made up of those who joined religious life after World War II; they are the Baby Boomers. After that group, fewer women joined religious communities. Unlike the Boomers, who were of a homogenous culture and identity, these new Gen-Xers and Millennials are more diverse. As the world becomes more multicultural, each community should become more accustomed to living interculturally.

Projecting into the future as a smaller community, we need a shared leadership that emphasizes every member as a leader and an operation based on collaboration and networking. Collaboration means that each community has access to others and can bring in information and share out resources. In the spirit of collaboration, networking should function as an essential tool to connect people around the globe.

In the twenty-first century, many people are worried about the future. We hear the cry of the poor, who live on the streets and are jobless, and the immigrants and exiles, who were uprooted and wander in foreign lands. We are facing an ecological crisis and extreme weather that threatens to make people and creatures extinct. We are a small and perhaps weak group, but God continuously calls our names, and we will continue this march. As much as possible, we should make friends with others and form various hybrid multiple subjectivities to create a new network to delink global capitalism's monopoly and relink people as family. In this global world, we women religious must stand hand in hand to embody our mission, which demands bringing the kingdom of heaven here and now.

In conclusion, I hold a strong hope for the future of apostolic religious life, rooted in our trust of God. Throughout this process of conversing, pondering, and writing, I have rekindled the hope that living into the diversity emerging in religious life—as well as crossing borders in every possible way—holds the promise of a vibrant future for religious life. Encounter means an embrace of the other, through which each deepens and extends the horizon of one's life and experiences liberation in a transformed way. Diversity can reenergize charisms among us. Like organic living systems, religious life is nourished and sustained by diversity. This new way requires skills of connection and communication that new generations will surely bring, and this web of connectivity and energy will surely influence our religious life.

Our mission will go forward into the global world of the twenty-first century. In the spirit of global sisterhood, women religious continue the march of the Jesus movement with a deep desire for freedom, and with all the sisters around the world in dialogue, learning together, to heed the call of the time.

The Question

The world that you will live in the future is rapidly changing. What kind of sisters do you want to work with in the future or—if you became a sister—what kind of sister would you want to be?

Response of Holy Names University Students to the Question:

I would like to work with a sister who is caring, loving, and motivated. However, she has to be strong. The sister must have been through life so that she understands that life is hard, but at the same time, she does not see it as an excuse to do wrong things. She has to have integrity and wisdom as well as a high level of emotional intelligence.

(I am religious to a certain extent.) I want to work with hardworking, patient, thoughtful, and helpful nuns. Also, the nun has to be nice and can crack a joke once or twice because the best way to learn is through having fun. Learning from people you respect is better.

Future sisters should be open-minded. They should be able to adapt to the evolving society. This is the only way that they can truly serve the community. They should also be kind, compassionate, and caring. Of course, to be a sister you must have these qualities embedded into your personality. The sisters of the past are long gone. Sisters should be driven to help their communities and adapt to their needs.

In the future, I would want to work with a sister who is loving and nonjudgmental. I would like for her to be supportive and caring of all people with no judgment. Also, I would probably prefer to work with a sister who is willing to help overlooked communities because that is what I hope to do in my career as well. So someone who is willing to put light with me into the darkest places.

The kinds of sisters that I would enjoy working with would have to be sisters that are proactive, positive, but also do not sugar-coat anything—the kind that I can rely on. I want them to love life and I want them to want to make society better as time goes on. Their lifestyle is their own and you can learn much from a person by the way they live and I want them to live how they want to. I want to teach them and I want them to teach me.

I want sisters who have a personality of caring and loving, sisters who care for the people around them, but sisters who care about their own well-being also. At the same time, I want the sisters to be able to have fun in their life while still being true to their vows. Also the sisters should have strong minds and be able to take any criticism from the people around them.

I am not religious, yet I understand that religion is something that cannot simply vanish. If I were a leader of society, I would want to work with someone who is open-minded yet logical. With a world like ours, we may not always see the good in things, yet we should not dwell only on the negative.

I want to work with women who are honest and strong. They will have to know what they want in life and what will make them happy regardless of what others think. I try to be like this myself, but it is hard to be honest with myself sometimes. It is easier to go with what everyone else is doing because that is easy. Women religious should show that women are strong and have integrity.

I would want to work with sisters who are understanding and knowledgeable of the situations that we face. I would want them to be sweet and kind, but also to be able to offer a level of discipline and respect. I would definitely want a sister who can somehow relate to certain situations, whether they are tough or just normal, so that she can be a model for others. In our generation, sisters are seen as out of touch and separate from everyone else, so sisters who are seen as any other average person would be beneficial.

I would want to be surrounded by sisters who are powerful and loving. They must have strength that will allow them to conquer any problem or task and do it with confidence and originality. I want women who aren't afraid to be themselves and are passionate about anything they desire. I want women who aren't negative and angry at the world. They must love and embrace everything around them. They look for the good in everything and want only love and success in their lives and the lives of those around them.

The sisters I would want to work with and enjoy would be those who are up to date with the generation. I understand that there are a lot of old traditions, but creating new ones, which the new generation could related to, would be great. Keeping a positive attitude as a sister is a must. She must be someone who is relatable and easy to talk to. NO ROOM FOR ANY JUDGEMENT! BUT ALL ROOM FOR UNDERSTANDING. Being a sister is being kind and loving.

If I were to be working closely with sisters in the future, I would want to see sisters who are strong, respected and understanding, spiritual, and who do not judge others for their different lifestyles. I think that as a Christian woman, it is easy to judge and discriminate against people with different beliefs and lifestyles, and I think it is important to accept everyone no matter what type of life other people live.

I would like to see sisters be more:
−understanding
−not judgmental
−not too strict and snippy when people make mistakes
−not act as if they are more important
−loving and caring toward everyone, not just people who are poor
−talkative
−expressive and genuine, not too proper or sophisticated
−fun and be Ok with having a personality of their own.

I want to work with a sister who is funny and caring and wants to listen to all our problems, good and bad. And I'm looking for a sister not to judge but to provide wisdom and discussion to help our struggles. Also, she should have a strong, independent mind and want to make changes in the world.

I want to work with a sister who would always listen to all opinions, who respects one another, and is honest, not hiding any secrets. I would want to see sisters who always help each other and help anyone who needs help. But the most important thing is for the sisters to enjoy their work or ministry.

In the future, I would want to see sisters who are kind, passionate, and accepting. I would like to see sisters who want to change the world for the better. I could imagine sisters who are passionate about social justice, willing to go against society to fight for what is right.

A sister who acknowledges the sins that the church and religion committed and is open to state that being gay or part of the LGBT is not sinful. They promote the idea that people are normal, not unique because of gender, race, color, identity, and sexuality. Stop being self-centered in religion (Christianity); there are different religions and beliefs. Be honest with others and yourself. Value truth.

The type of nun that I would like to work with would be a nun from the ages thirty-five to forty-five. A person who has a lot of life experiences; lived both a wealthy life and a troubled life. I would like to work with a very outgoing and understanding nun who gets along with everyone. I would also like to work with a nun who has lived in both generations, old and new.

The sisters I would like to work with in the future are ones who do not give up their dreams and aren't afraid of learning and trying different ways of finding their mystic hearts.

I would want to work with a sister who puts others before herself. I would enjoy working most with someone who is kind and has a big heart yet can still be strong and a little assertive. Someone who can be easily manipulated is not a good person to work with. I prefer to work with a person who has her own ideas and opinions on different topics. I would also like to work with someone who is not afraid to speak her mind.

In the future, I expect sisters to come from all walks of life. I want to see a diverse pool of women that tie the spiritual and social aspects together, while actively seeking to change a segment that is plagued with disparity. I expect sisters to be holistic thinkers without judgment, for they know their places in the world and do their utmost to avoid bias. They are well versed in realism and introspection.

I would want to work with sisters who know and understand people from other cultures and religions as well as keeping their passion for a global concern. Not just cold and aloof.

I would like to work with sisters who know many religions and cultures so that they truly work with immigrants.

If I were to be a sister, I would want to be a revolutionary while still devoting my time to God. I would be focused on changing society for the better in every aspect. I would shine a light on all people, no matter their background. We need more people fighting for minorities, the LGBTQ community, gun control, education, and so on. Open-mindedness and strong will are the traits I would have.

If I were to be a sister, I would like to love everyone equally. There are so many people who judge others and are only nice to people who are successful, rich, and have social status. Social issues I would want to work on are provision of education and guiding children in rough areas because a lot of them are born into a life of violence and gang environments. Often, they do not know how to do well in school, get a good job, and make good money. They do not receive the same education as the people in rich areas. If they got guidance and education, everyone would have equal opportunities.

If I were to be a nun, I would want to be a nun who can get rid of problems such as world hunger and poverty. The way I would carry myself is being very friendly and always being open to new ideas. I would like to take leadership, such as making sure to convince others to do the same. I would also have connections with big important people so that I could make a bigger impact in the world.

The kind of nuns I would like, if I were to work with them, would be open-minded ones. Ones that I could have in-depth conversations with about their beliefs and why they believed it. Also ones that could kind of be a mentor for me and help me figure out my spiritual journey. A nun that I could have a close relationship with and feel as though they were a friend but also someone to look up too as well.

A sister who is understanding of the world around her and understands that no two persons are alike. One that tries to help change the world but stays true to oneself. A nun that will stay focused on the task at hand and help others in need. A nun that is self-aware and is willing to help others to be aware of themselves without forcing them.

I would work with a nun who is more outgoing and social instead of being quiet and reserved all the time. I like learning about religion, and it is best for me to learn in an active and fun environment while being studious and an active listener.

I would want to be a nun or sister that looks to other religions with respect. Also we should be able to express the ideas of the Catholic Church without shame.

Bibliography

Achtemeier, Paul J. Joel Green, and Marianne Meye Thompson. *Introducing the New Testament: Its Literature and Theology*. Cambridge: Eerdmans, 2001.

Amin, Samir. *The Implosion of Contemporary Capitalism*. New York: Monthly Review, 2013.

Anzaldúa, Gloria. *Borderlands La Frontera: The New Mestiza*. San Francisco: Aunt Lute, 2007.

Aquino, Jorge A. "Mestizaje: The Latina/o Religious Imaginary in the North American Racial Crucible." In *The Wiley Blackwell Companion to Latino/a Theology*, edited by Orlando O Espin, 283–312. New York: Wiley, 2015.

Arnold, Simon Pedra. "Is there a Future for Consecrated Life?" Unpublished essay for the General Chapter of CCVI in 2017.

Aschroft, Bill, Garth Griffiths, and Helen Tiffin. *Post-Colonial Studies: The Key Concepts*. New York: Routledge, 1998.

Becker, Mary, and Mary Ondreyco. "What It's Like to Accompany Migrants at the U.S. Border." February 22, 2019. http://www.snjmusontario. org/2019/02/22/what-its-like-to-accompany-migrants-at-the-u-s-border/?fbclid=IwAR26G.

Bell, Catherine. *Ritual Theory; Theory Ritual*. New York: Oxford University Press, 1996.

Benezet, Julie. *The Journey of Not Knowing: How 21st Century Leaders Can Chart a Course Where There Is None*. Ashland, OR: Morton Hill, 2016.

Bentson, Lisa. *Focused Networking: The Eight Principles of 21st Century Marketing*. Bloomington: AuthorHouse, 2018.

Bevans, Steve. "God Inside Out: Notes toward a Missionary Theology of the Holy Spirit." https://sedosmission.org/old/eng/Bevans.html.

Bhabha, Homi. *The Location of Culture*. New York: Routledge, 1997.

Billings, Bradly S. "From House Church to Tenement Church: Domestic Space and the Development of early Urban Christianity—The Example of Ephesus." *Journal of Theological Studies* 62:2 (October 2011) 541–69.

"The Birthday Paradox." Wikipedia. http://www.en.m.wikipedia.org.

Bourbon, Julie. "Moving 'beyond the Wall': Immigration Panel Talks Moral, Practical Solutions." *National Catholic Reporter*, February 5, 2019. https://

www.ncronline.org/news/justice/moving-beyond-wall-immigration-panel-talks-moral-practical-solutions.

Brown, Raymond. *Introduction to the New Testament*. New York: Doubleday, 1997.

Brueggemann, Walter. "Prophetic Imagination: A Call to Leaders." In *Transformational Leadership: Conversations with the Leadership Conference of Women Religious*, edited by Annmarie Sanders, 68–80. Maryknoll: Orbis, 2015.

Catholic Health Association of the United States. https://www.chausa.org/about/about/our-history.

Cha, Therese Hak Kyoung. *The Dictee*. Berkeley: University of California Press, 2000.

Chittister, Joan. *The Fire in These Ashes: A Spirituality of Contemporary Religious Life*. Kansas City: Seed & Ward, 1995.

Choi, Suk Bon, et al. "Effects of Transformative and Shared Leadership Styles on Employees' Perception of Team Effectiveness." *Social Behavior and Personality* 45:3 (March 2017) 377–86.

"Chronicles of the Sisters of the Holy Names of Jesus and Mary. Oakland: 1868–1896." Holy Names University, unpublished manuscript.

Concluding Document: Aparecida, 13 a 31 de Mayo de 2007. Bogota, Columbia: Consejo Episcopal Latinoamericano, 2008.

Cossio, Hector. "A 40 años de la autopoiesis de Maturana, el concepto más revolucionario de la ciencia chilena a nivel mundial." *Elmo Strador*, November 27, 2013. http://www.elmostrador.cl/cultura/2013/11/27/a-cuarenta-anos-de-la-autopoiesis-de-maturana-el-concepto-mas-revolucionario-de-la-ciencia-chilena-a-nivel-mundial.

Dawn, Araujo-Hawkins. "Reckoning: White Sisters Respond to Their Racism, to One Historian's Call for Justice." *National Catholic Reporter*, January 8, 2018. https://www.ncronline.org/preview/reckoning-white-sisters-respond-their-own-racism-one-historians-call-justice.

Deck, Allan. *Francis: Bishop of Rome*. New York: Paulist, 2016.

Derrida, Jacques, and Anne Dufourmantelle. *Of Hospitality: Cultural Memory in the Present*. Translated by Rachel Bowlsby. Stanford, CA: Stanford University Press, 2000.

Elizondo, Virgilio. *The Future Is Mestizo: Life Where Cultures Meet*. Rev. ed. Boulder: University of Colorado Press, 2000.

———. *Galilean Journey: The Mexican American Promise: Journey to Liberation*. Rev. ed. New York: Orbis, 2000.

Ewens, Mary. *Removing the Veil: The Liberated American Nun in the 19th Century*. Center for the Study of American Catholicism, Working Paper Series 3. Notre Dame, IN: University of Notre Dame, 1978.

Fanon, Franz. *Black Skin, White Masks*. New York: Grove, 1967.

Feník, Jurah, and Robért Lapko. "Annunciation to Mary in Luke 1–2." *Biblica* 96:4 (2015) 498–524.

Fialka, John. *Sisters: Catholic Nuns and the Making of America.* New York: St. Martin's, 2003.

Fiand Barbara. *Refocusing the Vision.* New York: Crossroad, 2001.

Fisher, June. Letter to Sister Margaret Ellen (Mary Peter) Traxler. July 26, 1969. National Catholic Conference of Interracial Justice, series 4, box 3, Marquette University Archives.

Foundation of Life Women's Center. http://folptty.org/folw/.

Gallagher, Clarence. "The Church and the Institutes of Consecrated Life." *Way Supplement* 50 (Summer 1984) 3–15.

Gittins, Anthony J. *Living Mission Interculturally: Faith, Culture, and the Renewal of Praxis.* Collegeville, MN: Liturgical, 2010.

Glatz, Carol. "Number of Priest Declined for First Time in Decade, Vatican Says." *Crux*, March 6, 2019. https://cruxnow.com/vatican/2019/03/06/number-of-priests-declined-for-first-time-in-decade-vatican-says/.

Goehring, James. *Ascetics, Society and Desert: Study in Early Egyptian Monasticism.* Harrisburg, PA: Trinity, 1999.

Gonzalez, Justo L. *Acts: The Gospel of the Spirit.* Maryknoll: Orbis, 2001.

Graham, Kate Child. "Heeding Founder's Call: Women Religious Combat Racism." March 6, 2010. http://snddenjp.org/2010/03/06/heeding-founders-call-women-religious-combat-racism/.

Groom, Thomas. *What Makes Us Catholic: Eight Gifts for Life.* New York: HarperCollins, 2001.

Grubb, Sidnee, "Mariposa Ministries Creates Intentional Community with Refugee Women." *Global Sisters Report*, November 1, 2018. https://www.globalsistersreport.org/news/ministry/mariposa-ministries-creates-intentional-community-refugee-women-55554.

Hardt, Michael, and Antonio Negri, *Multitude: War and Democracy in the Age of Empire.* New York: Penguin, 2004

Harmer, Catherine M. *Religious Life in the 21st Century: A Contemporary Journey Into Canaan.* Mystic, CT: Twenty-Third, 1995.

"How Many Genders Are There?" https://www.quora.com/How-many-genders-are-there-in-human-beings.

International Organization for Migration. "Factsheet." http://www. gmdac.iom.int/global-migration-trends-factsheet.

Johnson, Mary, Patricia Wittberg, and Mary Gautier. *New Generations of Catholic Sisters: The Challenge of Mary Diversity.* New York: Oxford University Press, 2014.

Kinsey, Dinan. *Owed Justice: Thai Women Trafficked into Debt Bondage in Japan.* New York: Human Rights Watch, 2000.

Koehlinger, Amy L. *The New Nuns: Racial Justice and Religious Reform in the 1960s.* Cambridge, MA: Harvard University Press, 2007.

Kohls, Sarah. "Something Old, Something New: Hanna's Vow (I Sam 1–2) Touches the Lives of Women Religious Today." In *In Our Own Words: Religious Life in a Changing World*, edited by Juliet Mousseau and Sarah Kohles, 18–30. Collegeville, MN: Liturgical, 2018.

Kristeva, Julia. *Strangers to Ourselves*. Translated by Leon S. Roudiez. New York: Columbia University Press, 1995.

Kwok, Puilan. *Introducing Asian Feminist Theology*. Cleveland, OH: Pilgrim, 2000.

Lacan, Jacques. *Anxiety*. Edited by Jacques-Alain Miller, translated by A. R. Price. The Seminar of Jacques Lacan, Book X. Malden: Polity, 2016.

———. *The Four Fundamental Concepts of Psychoanalysis*. Edited by Jacques-Alain Miller, translated by Alan Sheridan. The Seminar of Jacques Lacan, Book XI. New York: Norton, 1978.

Lao Tzu. *Tao Te Ching*. Translated by James Legge. http://classics.mit.edu/Lao/taote.mb.txt.

LCWR. "History." https://www. lcwr.org/about/history.

Lee, Archie C. C. "The Bible in Chinese Christianity: Its Reception and Appropriation in China." *Ecumenical Review*, March, 2015, 96–106.

Massa, Mark. *Anti-Catholicism in America: The Last Acceptable Prejudice*. New York: Crossroad, 2003.

Massingale, Bryan. *Racial Justice and the Catholic Church*. Maryknoll, NY: Orbis, 2010.

Matovina, Timothy. *Latino Catholicism: Transformation in America's Largest Church*. Princeton, NJ: Princeton University Press, 2012.

Mavelli, Luca, and Erin K. Wilson. *The Refugee Crisis and Religion: Secularism, Security and Hospitality in Question*. New York: Rowman & Littlefield, 2017.

Maya, Teresa. "Called to Leadership: Challenges and Opportunities for Younger Members in Leadership." In *Our Own Words: Religious Life in a Changing World*, edited by Juliet Mousseau and Sarah Kohles, 159–81. Collegeville, MN: Liturgical, 2018.

McNamara, Jo Ann Kay. *Sisters in Arms: Catholic Nuns through Two Millennia*. Cambridge, MA: Harvard University Press, 1996.

Meilander, Gilbert. "Friendship in the Classical World." *First Things*, May 1999. https://www.firstthings.com/article/1999/05/friendship-in-the-classical-world.

Metzger, Bruce M. *A Textual Commentary on the Greek New Testament*. 2nd ed. Edmonds: Deutsche Bibelgesellschaft/German Bible Society, 1998.

Miller, Trevor. "Understanding Desert Monasticism." https://www.northumbriacommunity.org/articles/understanding-desert-monasticism/.

Min, Anselm Kyoungsuk. *The Solidarity of Others in a Divided World: A Postmodern Theology after Postmodernism*. New York: T. & T. Clark, 2004.

National Catholic Educational Association. "Brief History." https://www.ncea.org/NCEA/About_Us/NCEA/About/About_Us.aspx?hkey=5470d2fe-6f67-4aae-8b5b-4385a9a39082.

Neal, Marie Augusta. *From Nuns to Sisters: An Expanding Vocation*. Mystic, CT: Twenty-Third, 1990.

O'Murchu, Diarmuid. *Consecrated Religious Life: The Changing Paradigms*. Maryknoll, NY: Orbis, 2005.

———. *Poverty, Celibacy, and Obedience.* New York: Crossroad, 1999.

———. *Religious Life in the 21st Century: The Prospect of Refounding.* Maryknoll, NY: Orbis, 2016.

Park, Jung Eun Sophia. *A Hermeneutic on Dislocation as Experience: Creating a Borderland, Constructing a Hybrid Identity.* New York: Peter Lang, 2011.

———. "Jesus of Minjung on the Road to Emmaus (Luke 24:13–32): Envisioning a Post-Minjung Theology." In *Jesus of Galilee: Contextual Christology for the 21st Century,* edited by Bob Lassalle-Klein, 149–59. New York: Orbis, 2010.

———. "Religious Life in the U.S.: A Vocation of Border Crossing." *New Theology Review* 27:1 (September 2014) 47–53.

———. "St. Clare—Woman of Today: Revisited Theme of Apostolic Freedom." *Theology and Thought* 30:2 (June 2010) 219–45.

Pellegrino, Mary. "'The Future Enters Us Long before It Happens: Opening Space for an Emerging Narrative of Communion." https://lcwr.org/sites/default/files/calendar/attachments/2017_lcwr_presidential_address_-_mary_pellegrino_csj.pdf.

Perfectae Caritas (Decree on the Up-to-Date Renewal of Religious life). In *The Documents of Vatican Council II: The Conciliar and Post Conciliar Documents,* edited by Austin Falnnery. New rev. ed. Boston: St. Paul, 1992.

Peters, Edward N. *The 1917 or Pio-Benedictine Code of Canon Law in English Translation.* San Francisco: Ignatius, 2001.

Pieterse, Nederveen. *Globalization and Culture: Global Mélange.* 2nd ed. Lanham, MD: Rowman & Littlefield, 2009.

Pope Francis. "Discurso del papa Francisco en La Ceremonia de Acogida y Apertura de la JMJ Panama 2019." *Aciprensa,* January 24, 2019. https://www.aciprensa.com/noticias/ceremonia-de-acogida-y-apertura-de-la-jmjen-el-campo-santa-maria-la-antigua-24189.

———. "For a Culture of Encounter." Morning meditation, Chapel of the Domus Sanctae Marthae, September 13, 2016. https://w2.vatican.va/content/francesco/en/cotidie/2016/documents/papa-francesco-cotidie_20160913_for-a-culture-of-encounter.html.

———. Homily, Holy Saturday, Vatican Basilica, April 19, 2014." http://w2.vatican.va/content/francesco/en/homilies/2014/documents/papa-francesco_20140419_omelia-veglia-pasquale.html.

———. "Homily of Pope Francis." Radio Vaticana, July 22, 2016. http://es.radiovaticana.va/news/2016/07/22/prefacio_-_papa_francisco_-_libro_madre_teresa/1246066.

Reclaiming Jesus. "Confession of Faith in a Time of Crisis." http://www.reclaimingjesus.org/ and https://sojo.net/media/reclaiming-jesus-speaking-integrity-our-faith.

Resource Center for Religious Institutes. "Q and A's—Commissary for Religious Institutes." *News in Brief* 10:2 (2018) 4–6.

Rieger, Joerg. *Christ & Empire: From Paul to Postcolonial Times.* Minneapolis: Fortress, 2007.

Rumi, Jellaludin. "The Guest House." http://www.sagemindfulness.com/blog/rumi-s-poem-the-guest-house.

Sánchez, Mercedes Leticia Casas. "Introduction: Inspirational Guidelines (Horizonte Inspirador)." http://www.clar.org/plan-global.html.

Sanders, Annmarie, editor. *Transformational Leadership: Conversations with the Leadership Conference of Women Religious.* Maryknoll, NY: Orbis, 2015.

Savelle, Charles H. "A Reexamination of the Prohibitions in Acts 15." *Bibliotheca Sacra* 161 (October–December 2004) 449–68.

Scanon, Sydney. "Liminal Space." https://www.powerpoetry.org/poems/liminal-space.

Schaberg, Jane. "Luke." In *Women's Bible Commentary: Expanded Edition with Apocrypha*, edited by Carol Newsom and Sharon Ringe, 363–80. Louisville: Westminster John Knox, 1998.

Schneiders, Sandra. *Buying the Field: Catholic Religious Life in Mission to the World, Religious Life in a New Millennium.* Vol. 3. New York: Paulist, 2013.

———."Christian Spirituality as an Academic Discipline." *Christian Spirituality Bulletin* (1994) 25–34.

———. *Prophets in Their Own Country: Women Religious Bearing Witness to the Gospel in a Troubled Church.* Maryknoll, NY: Orbis, 2011.

———. *The Revelatory Text*, 2nd edition. Collegeville, MN: Liturgical, 1999.

———. *That Was Then . . . This Is Now: The Past, Present, and Future of Women Religious in the United States.* Notre Dame, IN: Center for Spirituality, 2011.

———. *Written That You May Believe: Encountering Jesus in the Fourth Gospel.* New York: Herder, 1999.

Schreck, Nancy. "However Long the Night: Holy Mystery Revealed in Our Midst." Keynote address, Leadership Conference of Women Religious, August 2014. https://lcwr.org/sites/default/files/calendar/attachments/however_long_the_night_-_nancy_schreck_osf_final_0.pdf.

Schumacher, E. F. *Small Is Beautiful: Economic as If People Mattered.* New York: Harper & Row, 1973.

Shirky, Clay. *Here Come Everybody: The Power of Organizing Without Organizations.* New York: Penguin, 2008.

Silverstein, Shel. "This Bridge." In *A Light in the Attic*, 168. New York: HarperCollins, 1989.

Sinek, Simon. *Leaders Eat Last: Why Some Teams Pull Together and Others Don't.* New York: Penguin, 2014.

Sivalon, John. "The Gift of Uncertainty." *The Occasional Papers: The Leadership Conference of Women Religious*, Winter 2015, 12–15.

Smith, Simon, and Joseph G Donders, editors. *Refugees Are People: An Action Report on the Refugees in Africa.* Eldoret, Kenya: Gaba, 1985.

Spivak, Gayatri Chakravorty. "Foreword: Upon Reading the Companion to Postcolonial Studies." In *A Companion to Postcolonial Studies*, edited by Henry Schwarz and Sangeeta Ray. New York: Blackwell, 2000.

Strauss, Ilana E. "The Hot New Millennial Housing Trend Is a Repeat of the Middle Ages." *The Atlantic*, September 26, 2016. https://www.theatlantic. com/business/archive/2016/09/millennial-housing-communal-living-middle-ages/501467/.

Suzuki, David. "From Ecosystems to Species to Cultures, Diversity Is Key to Survival." *AlterNet*, August 31, 2016. https://www.alternet.org/ environment/ecosystems-species-cultures-diversity-key-survival.

Tan, Amy. *The Joy Luck Club*. New York: Ivy, 1989.

UNESCO. "Universal Declaration on Cultural Diversity." November 2, 2001. http://portal.unesco.org/en/ev.phpURL_ID=13179&URL_DO=DO_ TOPIC&URL_SECTION=201.html.

United Nations. "Trafficking in Human Beings." http://www.unodc.org/unodc/ em/trafficking_human_beings_.html.

USCCB. "History of Hispanic Ministry." http://www.usccb.org/issues-and-action/cultural-diversity/hispanic-latino/resources/history-of-hispanic-ministry-in-the-united-states.cfm.

———. "New Study On Cultural Diversity Displays Catholic Church's Growing Multicultural Parish Population." November 15, 2016. http://www.usccb. org/news/2016/16-154.cfm.

Varia, Nisha. "The Hidden Victims of Human Trafficking." *Human Right Watch*, June 29, 2011. https://www.hrw.org/news/2011/06/29/hidden-victims-human-trafficking.

Vattamattam, Matthew. "Intercutural Community Living." July 2, 2012. http:// www.claretianformation.com/intercultural-community-living/.

Weibel, Peter. "People, Politics, and Power." In *Global Activism: Art and Conflict in the 21st Century*, edited by Peter Weibel, 29–34. Cambridge, MA: MIT Press, 2014.

White, Michael L. "The Jesus Movement: How Jesus' Followers Responded in the Traumatic Days Following His Death." Frontline, April 1998. https:// www.pbs.org/wgbh/pages/frontline/shows/religion/first/themovement. html.

Wiseman, Liz. *Multipliers: How the Best Leaders Make Everyone Smarter*. New York: Harper Business, 2010.

Wohlleben, Peter. *The Hidden Life of Trees: What They Feel, How They Communicate*. British Columbia, Canada: Greystone, 2016.

Yakupitiyaga, Thanranga. "Recorded Increase in Human Trafficking, Women and Girls Targeted." *Inter Press Service*, January 9, 2019. http://www. ipsnews.net/2019/01/recorded-increase-human-trafficking-women-girls-targeted/.

Young, Frances M. *Biblical Exegesis and The Formation of Christian Culture*. Cambridge: Cambridge University Press, 1997.